Themes
from
Acts

Paul E. Pierson

Regal Books A Division of GL Publications
Ventura, CA U.S.A.

Other good reading:

Highlights of the Bible: New Testament by William Lane

Life As It Was Meant to Be by Lloyd John Ogilvie (1 and 2 Thessalonians)

Eternity in Their Hearts by Don Richardson

The foreign language publishing of all Regal books is under the direction of Gospel Literature International (GLINT). GLINT provides financial and technical help for the adaptation, translation and publishing of books for millions of people worldwide. For information regarding translation, contact: GLINT, P.O. Box 6688, Ventura, California 93006.

Published by Regal Books
A Division of GL Publications
Ventura, California 93006
Printed in U.S.A.

Library of Congress Cataloging in Publication Data
Pierson, Paul Everett.
   Themes from Acts.

   (Bible commentary for laymen)
   Bibliography: p.
   1. Bible. N.T. Acts—Commentaries.   I. Title.
II. Series.
BS2625.3.P53   226'.607   82-80153
ISBN 0-8307-0819-7   AACR2

Contents

A Teacher's Manual and Student Discovery Guide for Bible study groups using this book are available from your church supplier.

Acknowledgement

Much of the material in this study was first given in a series of sermons in the First Presbyterian Church of Fresno, California, where I served as pastor from 1973 to 1980. It seems that one always receives more than he gives in a healthy relationship and this one was no exception. Many in that congregation were like Barnabas in the early church, standing alongside each other and their pastors to encourage, counsel, and support them in a shared ministry. Because of their genuine desire to be responsive to God's call, their deep sense of *koinonia,* and their growing missionary vision, my family and I owe more to the people of that congregation than we can ever fully express.

Introduction

About two-thirds of the way through the first century, a remarkable two-volume work began to circulate among the Christian communities of the Roman Empire. It was written by a meticulous historian, a careful researcher familiar with the geography and life of the Mediterranean world, who was an eyewitness to many of the events he narrated. His was an ambitious undertaking. He set out to describe, for believers as well as nonbelievers, the origin and growth of the Christian faith from an obscure village in far-off Palestine, to Rome, the political and geographical center of the ancient world. His work pointed to the day when the Faith would be carried beyond Rome to every corner of the earth.

Because of the unanimous opinion that both volumes were written by Luke, the companion of Paul, the first is known to us simply as the Gospel of Luke. The other has been called, since the second century, the Acts of the Apostles. But it is essential to remember that the central figure in both is Jesus Christ. In Luke He is the Incarnate Son of God, with us in the flesh; in Acts He is the risen Christ, acting powerfully through the Holy Spirit to bring God's salvation and reconciliation and new life to all who will receive Him, calling His disciples to participate with Him in this mission.

The book of Acts is many things. It is one of the most exciting adventure tales ever written. And why not, since it was written by the Holy Spirit in the lives of men and women gripped by the risen Christ! From the Spirit-filled disciples at Pentecost to Paul teaching in a Roman prison, we see violent mob scenes, stonings, shipwrecks, prison escapes and earthquakes, interspersed with healings, visions, trials and sermons in the most unlikely places. It is also a portrait of the early church. We hear its basic message proclaimed, we see a new life-style emerge, we encounter power and courage. And with it we find fear, halfhearted faith, greed, conflict and the struggle to understand the Faith; these believers were all too human. But these ordinary people did extraordinary things as they responded to the risen Christ.

Above all, Acts makes it clear that God has a purpose for His people within history and a strategy for them to follow. His purpose, promised to Abraham nearly two thousand years earlier, is that "all peoples on earth will be blessed through you" (Gen. 12:3) with the message of redemption and life. His strategy, demonstrated frequently in the book, is that men and women, called by the Holy Spirit and supported by the church, would cross every kind of barrier—geographical, cultural, linguistic, and religious—which prevents others from hearing the Good News, going to them and inviting them to discipleship. Here we see the first steps in working out this strategy and hear a call to become participants ourselves.

Acts is an incomplete book, an unfinished symphony. Its incompleteness stands as a call to every believer today to adopt for his own the goal given to the Messiah, "that you may bring my salvation to the ends of the earth" (Isa. 49:6).

As we discover what God did in and through the

early church, may we also discover what He wills to do in and through us today. With that discovery will come the confidence that He surely will if we are open and responsive to His voice. For it is the same God who calls us, the same risen Christ who goes ahead of us and the same Holy Spirit who empowers us as we follow.

CHAPTER ONE

Jerusalem: The First Circle

Acts 1:1-26

Acts is a continuation of the gospel story. Now that it was clear to the disciples that Jesus had indeed risen from the dead, what did it mean? What were the implications for the disciples, for Israel, for the world? Clearly, they were staggering. This event would shape human destiny and world history as no other. But how?

Before Luke related how God led His people further in understanding their new life and mission, he oriented his readers by going back to his first volume. He again addressed Theophilus, whose name meant "lover of God" or "loved by God." Since Theophilus was not a Jew, he served as a symbol pointing to all those of other races, cultures and religions to whom the Good News would be taken. Thus he pointed to the major theme of the book.

From Luke we learn that Jesus appeared to His disciples over a period of 40 days between His resurrection and ascension. Here we discover that the theme of His teaching during that time continued the central thrust of His ministry prior to the cross. He led them more deeply into the Old Testament Scriptures to an understanding, not only of His Messiahship, but of the Kingdom of God. We are sure He explained to them how the Messiah was to be the "Suffering Servant," depicted in Isaiah 52 and 53, and that He could not fulfill

His mission and bring in the Kingdom otherwise. We are equally sure He led them into passages like Genesis 12:3, 22:18 and 26:4, where blessing to all the peoples on earth had been set forth as God's purpose from the beginning of redemptive history. His exposition of Isaiah must have focused also on texts like 42:6 and 49:6, where the prophet saw the worldwide dimensions of salvation, and 53:11,12, where "the many" clearly referred to other people and nations.

By telling us that his previous work dealt with "all that Jesus began to do and to teach" (Acts 1:1), the author made it clear that our Lord's redemptive work in human history was not over. Indeed it had only begun. Soon it would become apparent that God's plan was to continue that ministry through a special people whom He would call to Himself. Paul would later refer to them as the Body of Christ, an amazing, even presumptuous image if not true. It suggested that God's people were not only recipients of His blessings but participants in His mission, and that one could not be separated from the other. But how was that to come about? How could very ordinary, fallible people continue the ministry of Jesus Christ? Two more clues, which would become major emphases in Acts, would answer the question.

The first clue was the resurrection. When Luke mentioned the many convincing proofs that Jesus was alive, he stressed the foundation of all Christian faith and action. Not only apostolic history, but all effective Christian life and thought would be built on the conviction that Jesus had risen from the dead and was fully as alive, powerful and accessible now as He had been during His days in Galilee. It was the risen Christ, not a mere memory, who would remain with His people, giving them life, power and purpose.

The other was the promise of the Holy Spirit. Known to the prophets of old, completely filling the

Incarnate Son, promised as a gift to His followers, He would soon be poured out in dimensions never before known. With the gift of the Spirit, God would make it possible for ordinary people to become participants in His extraordinary mission to the world.

The Agenda for the Church: Witness to the World

The disciples were all Jews, no doubt born and raised in Palestine. From childhood they had known the Old Testament Scriptures, focusing on those which promised restoration of the Kingdom to Israel. With all other Jews of their day they believed such restoration to be the mission of the Messiah. Even though Jesus had often told them and demonstrated by His actions that God's love extended far beyond the historic chosen people, the lesson had not penetrated their consciousness. We should not think this unusual. Jesus had told them very clearly at least three times that He would be rejected and killed and that He would rise again, but they had not understood or believed Him. How often have we failed to hear some truth from Scripture or a friend simply because certain preconceptions, prejudices or our own private agenda prevented it from taking root in our consciousness?

So it was with the disciples. Despite all of Jesus' teaching they still thought in narrow, ethnocentric terms, still believing that His mission was to restore the Kingdom to Israel. Their only question was timing. They believed God's primary concern was their own people. If others were to share in His blessings, it would be in a secondary sense. Their attitude was like that of many Christians of other times and places who have been only too happy to receive God's gifts, but who, having received them, thought little about passing them on to others. Could it be that contemporary

American Christians have fallen into the same fallacy? Do we assume that because God has blessed us so abundantly He must love us more and others less? Are we not in terrible danger of falling into the sin of Israel, seeing God's blessings as a right instead of a privilege which brings responsibility?

Jesus gently but firmly shifted the focus of the disciples' question and in a few words expanded their vision to include all peoples on earth. First, He dismissed the question of when God would fully establish His Kingdom. His people are not to speculate over the matter. They are to be obedient! Then in a few words our Lord gave the purpose and direction, not only of the apostles' ministry, but of all the subsequent history of the church. Luke uses these words as the theme, almost a table of contents, for Acts. "You will receive power when the Holy Spirit comes on you; and you will be my witnesses in Jerusalem, and in all Judea and Samaria, and to the ends of the earth" (Acts 1:8).

The followers of Christ, empowered by the Holy Spirit, are to take the Good News across every kind of barrier to every ethnic group on earth, until in each one there are those who worship and serve the God and Father of our Lord Jesus Christ. Jerusalem, Judea, Samaria and to the ends of the earth! These words symbolized the breaking of an almost infinite number of barriers in order that men and women everywhere might hear and respond to the Good News. Just as God in Christ had broken through the barriers which separated eternity from time, divinity from humanity, holiness from sin, so His people were to break through geographical, racial, linguistic, religious, cultural and social barriers in order that people of every race and tongue might receive the Good News.

It is easy to imagine that Jesus stooped down and began to draw a series of concentric circles in the sand as He spoke. The inner circle represented Jerusalem, where Jesus had concluded His public ministry, where He had been crucified and had risen from the dead. Witness in Jerusalem would be near-neighbor evangelism, telling the Good News to other Jews who spoke the same language, shared the Old Testament hope of the Messiah and had the same view. But there were barriers to be broken even here. The barrier of fear which surrounded the disciples themselves, the deep conviction that one condemned by the Jewish authorities and crucified could not be the Messiah, and the suspicion and hostility which normally greet that which is new. These and other barriers would always separate faith and unbelief.

However even in Jerusalem there was another kind of Jew. Alongside the Aramaic-speaking Palestinians there were Greek-speaking Jews, or Hellenists, who had been born and raised outside of Palestine. They were called the Jews of the Diaspora. They worshiped in separate synagogues and at times there was hostility between the two groups. Despite their greater openness to people of other cultures, the Hellenists shared the preconceptions and prejudices of the Palestinians against the new message. Only the Holy Spirit, beginning at Pentecost, would sweep men and women from both groups into the infant church.

The second circle represented Judea, the small geographical area surrounding Jerusalem which Pontius Pilate ruled in the name of Rome. The composition of the people was similar to that of Jerusalem, the barriers to be crossed the same as those in the capital city. The only additional one was that of distance. Judea will always stand as a reminder to the church that it must evangelize those beyond its own doorstep and neighborhood, who speak the same language and share the same culture, but have not yet heard or believed the

Good News of our Lord Jesus Christ.

For the apostles the third circle, representing Samaria, involved the smashing of a far more difficult barrier. Because of factors which lay buried in centuries of history, the Samaritans were despised by the Jews as racially impure religious heretics and traditional enemies. We recall the astonishment of the disciples when they found Jesus talking with a Samaritan woman and remember the eagerness with which James and John suggested Jesus call lightning down from heaven on a Samaritan village. Nevertheless, it was to Samaria that Jesus sent His disciples with the message of salvation. The barriers to be crossed were not only geographical, they were religious and sociological, but He bade them go to this traditionally despised people. Samaritans stand as a symbol of people who, although nearby, are seen as different, despised because of racial, cultural or religious differences.

Beyond the first three circles, Jesus drew for us an almost infinite series of additional concentric circles, as He sent the disciples to be His witnesses to the ends of the earth. Included in these circles there would be Asians, Europeans, Africans, Greeks and Romans; slaves and freemen; cultured and barbarians; of every race and language known to the Graeco-Roman world and all those beyond it. To carry the gospel to the ends of the earth was the major task that Jesus left to His church until He would come again. The book of Acts describes for us only the beginning of that process, not its end. Indeed its incompleteness stands as a mandate for the church to continue and complete the task.

Another helpful way of looking at Acts is in terms of a geographical schematic. As we look at a map of the Mediterranean world, Jerusalem is on our right. It was a provincial capital, despised by the Roman officials stationed there; it was also the city of David, the greatest of Jewish kings and an ancestor of the Messiah. But the news of the Messiah could not be limited to Jerusalem or to the Jews. Rome, where Acts ends, was clearly the political, economic and geographical center. That city, to which all roads led, was an important symbol. If the gospel was to be a universal message, it had to be taken to Rome. Although we know the faith was spread in other directions as well, Luke traces in Acts how the Good News was taken from Jerusalem to Rome. There the book ends abruptly.

However, we know that in the mind of Paul, the chief protagonist of Acts, Rome was not the end. It was his dream and hope that after visiting Rome he could go on to Spain. The Roman church was to become the base for the launching of a missionary effort to that land. And what did Spain represent on our map? Both the end and the beginning. The end of the Mediterranean world, its westernmost point and the entrance to the world beyond.

High on a hill overlooking Lisbon, Portugal, stands the castle of Saint George. Built up by a whole series of conquerors through the centuries, the city was first fortified by the Phoenicians who arrived there a century before the time of Christ. Thus we know that before the time of Paul, Palestinian sailors already had moved beyond the gates of Hercules (Gibraltar) into the Atlantic, turning north up the European coast. We do not know how much of the world Paul was aware of, but we can be sure he knew there was more beyond the Mediterranean basin. Thus it is not farfetched to believe that both in the mind of our Lord and in that of His greatest apostle, there burned a desire to carry the message beyond the Mediterranean basin and out into the world beyond.

The Ascension and the Holy Spirit

After Jesus had given this mandate to His disciples,

Luke wrote, "he was taken up . . . and a cloud hid him from their sight" (Acts 1:9). We should not think that Luke's account presupposes a flat earth as some have said. Rather it is God's way of symbolizing for us three important facts at this transition point in the history of salvation. First, it meant the vindication of all that Jesus had done and taught while on earth. His ascension to the right hand of the Father meant that He who had been born in a manger, was crucified and raised from the dead, was now at the seat of authority. He was declared Lord of history, to whom every knee would bow. His followers could trust Him completely both within and beyond history.

Secondly, the ascension symbolized the end of the first phase of Jesus' ministry: His life in the flesh, localized among one people in one place. Now the second stage of His ministry would begin. This new phase would be universal, extending to all peoples and places. The first phase had ended in the cross and resurrection; the second would not end until His Kingdom was completely established on earth. Thus the ascension implied the promise of His return, His total triumph over a world that would finally recognize Him, and the establishment of His Kingdom on earth at the end of history.

Thirdly, it pointed to His immediate return to His people in the person of the Holy Spirit. The Spirit, to use one of Paul's terms, is a "down payment," both a guarantee that the Kingdom will indeed come as was promised by the Scriptures, while the new quality of relationships and life which the Spirit brings are a foretaste of that promised Kingdom.

The Holy Spirit and Jesus Christ. The Spirit of God, known in special situations in the Old Testament and uniquely concentrated in the person of Jesus the Messiah, would soon be poured out on the messianic community, the church. Luke, with his universal missionary vision, was especially concerned to stress the continuity of the Spirit's work from the beginning of Jesus' life to the end of the narrative. From Jesus' birth in Bethlehem to Paul's ministry in Rome, we see the activity of the same Holy Spirit. First the Spirit showed us the nature of the salvation offered by Jesus; then He led an empowered church in spreading the Good News.

Because the Holy Spirit is the Spirit of Jesus, our Lord is the unique dispenser of that Spirit. The risen Christ Himself would fulfill His promise, made before the crucifixion and after the resurrection, by pouring Him out on His people. In turn the Holy Spirit would universalize the presence of the risen Christ. No longer would Jesus be limited by space and time as He had been during the days of His flesh. Now the disciples could live in a relationship with Christ even more intimate than they had enjoyed before. And that privilege would extend to all of Christ's disciples to the end of time and the ends of the earth. The Paraclete, the One called alongside, who had dwelt *with* them, would now dwell *within* them (see John 14:16).

The gift of the Spirit. There is much to be said about the Holy Spirit. In the passage at hand we see three essential aspects. First of all the Holy Spirit is a gift of God, freely given to all believers. He is poured out on all who repent and believe the gospel. The reality of this gift does not depend on any certain type of experience. Just as those who encountered Jesus during His days on earth had many diverse experiences, depending upon their own particular needs and unique personalities, so it will be among the followers of Jesus today.

It is a serious mistake to believe we receive the Holy Spirit only when we have a certain kind of spiritual experience. It is still more in error to believe that we bring on an experience of the Holy Spirit by our own striving. Nor is it wise to focus primarily on the gifts of the Spirit. Both the experience the Spirit may bring to us and the gifts He may give us are of immense value. But neither is the essence of the baptism of the Spirit. The essential gift of the Spirit is that God the giver, the risen Christ, is Himself the gift to us. He comes to dwell within us. That is the fundamental gift of the Christian life. All other gifts are secondary to this one.

Because the Christian life is a pilgrimage with the living Lord who dwells within us by His Spirit, it is a never-ending, multifaceted relationship. Like a good marriage, it is one that never stops growing in understanding, intimacy and responsiveness to the other. As the Spirit brings us into a growing relationship with Christ and we are drawn closer to Him, our lives are shaped more and more by His purpose for us as individuals and for the world. Thus Acts emphasizes not so much a particular experience of the Holy Spirit, but responsiveness to the Spirit as He led His people into mission to the ends of the earth.

Secondly, the Holy Spirit is given for one specific purpose above all others—to equip the disciples for ministry and mission. Of course He would be given to bring a new quality of life to believers and to create a new community, the church. But His fundamental purpose was to launch the church out into the continuation of Jesus' own mission in the world. We are used to thinking of the Spirit's ministry as primarily internal, within our personal lives and within the fellowship of the church. However, beginning in Acts 1:8 and continuing to the end of the book, Luke makes it clear that the Spirit's ministry is primarily outward, equipping believers, then leading them to new places and peoples to share the gospel.

When the Spirit came at Pentecost, the disciples would be enabled to witness to Jews from every nation in the empire: special manifestations of the Spirit would lead Philip to the Samaritans and to the Ethiopian; the Spirit would send a reluctant Peter to Cornelius, a Roman; and the Spirit would send Paul and Barnabas on the first organized missionary venture. At every point of advance across a new barrier in Acts, it was the Holy Spirit who took the initiative, sending His people beyond the place where they had settled down, preparing and empowering them as they responded.

Thirdly, the Spirit is the giver of power in order that God's people may fulfill His purpose in and through His church. Bertrand Russell wrote that man's whole life is controlled by the urge to gain power and glory, above all to gain power over his fellowman. More important than the drive for basic necessities, this one is insatiable, he said. The pursuit of power is like a gold rush. Men forget all else and go crazily forward to their doom.

But the power of the Spirit is totally different. Because it is the power of the risen Christ, it will always be consistent both with the way in which Jesus acted while on earth and with His purpose in history. In the ministry of Jesus we see love and power consistently combined. Above all, this is true in the cross and resurrection. At no other point in history do love and power come together as they do at Calvary and the empty tomb!

As we seek to understand the power of the Holy Spirit, we do well to examine how Jesus used His power. It always had a twofold purpose: to restore human life to all God created it to be in relationship to Himself and to glorify the Father in the process. So the power of the Holy Spirit would normally be directed toward the world in such a manner that men and women would put their trust in their Saviour, Jesus Christ, and become new persons as a result. Never manipulative or destructive, except of evil, we see this power manifested in a great variety of ways throughout Acts.

The apostles, empowered by the Spirit, would communicate the gospel across barriers of language, suspicions and hostility. They would glorify God by healing the sick. Frequently this power would enable believers to overcome their natural fears, prejudices and selfishness, leading them to act in a way that seemed contrary to their own best interests, as normally defined. Thus they gave away their possessions to care for those who had been strangers a short time earlier; they confronted demonic forces and overcame them; they defied rulers, faced death and even forgave their assassins. They broke through barriers of racial, religious and cultural differences as ancient enemies came together in the new messianic community.

At times the power of God released apostles from prison in miraculous circumstances, bringing men to glorify Him. At times His servants were allowed to die, but still to glorify God. The power of the Holy Spirit was no guarantee of safety, much less of ease. But it did assure God's people that they would be enabled to take the gospel to the ends of the earth. The Spirit was both a foretaste and a guarantee of the ultimate triumph of the risen Lord.

Witness and the Message

Witness is another key word in Acts, used in one form or another over 30 times in the book. In chapter 1 we read first that the apostles were to be witnesses of Jesus, then with the newly chosen Matthias they were to be witnesses of His resurrection. This gives us important clues, both as to the nature and content of Christian witness.

Clearly a witness is someone who speaks from firsthand experience, who describes something he has seen. To speak of a secondhand witness is a contradiction in terms. Thus the apostles were to tell of a person whom they had known and events they had witnessed. This was the specific objective content of their testimony. It focused on the person Jesus, what He had taught and done during His sojourn on earth, and above all, on who He was and is. The first point of their witness was that He was the long-awaited Messiah, the One who fulfilled the Scriptures, the Son of God.

The second point of their witness would go further. Jesus had not only been crucified, He had risen from the dead! His resurrection had validated His person and ministry. It had shown God's seal of approval on all He had said and done.

The third point of Christian witness went beyond the objective focus of the coming of Jesus, His death and resurrection. It shared the significance of Jesus for human life and history. They had heard the explanation of our Lord Himself after the resurrection; now the Holy Spirit would lead them to understand its meaning more deeply. Thus the apostles would begin to proclaim the life-changing and history-shaping significance of that event.

The life, death and resurrection of Jesus Christ was not a mere religious idea to be set alongside the many other religious and philosophical ideas of the Roman Empire. It was the unique invasion of the Creator into His world to reveal Himself and to redeem mankind. Henceforth the quality of life as well as the eternal destiny of men and women would be determined by their response to this crucified and resurrected Lord. History would one day find its consummation in His Kingdom to be established on earth. Was it any wonder that the apostles could not keep this message to themselves? Any wonder that they were compelled, almost against their will, to share it with the world?

But how are believers today to be genuine witnesses of Christ as the apostles were? Does not the very firsthand nature of authentic witness necessarily eliminate us? After all, we were not there with Jesus in Galilee and did not see Him crucified. Nearly two thousand years separate us from His resurrection! Can our witness or even our faith ever be anything other than secondhand?

The answer lies in two gifts: the first is the apostolic witness inspired and brought to us by the Holy Spirit in the New Testament; the second is the Spirit Himself, Christ in us, who comes to us through that Word. We first encounter the uniquely attractive person, Jesus, in Scripture. We watch Him heal and forgive; accept all kinds of people; we see Him crucified; we hear the news that He has risen from the dead. As we give ourselves to Him we are led into our own death and resurrection. We experience His power and action within us. He is no longer just a person in history. He is present in our lives. Our witness no longer merely points back to Christ in history; it now proclaims also the Christ who is alive and active today.

Thus with the apostles, we share the Good News of Jesus. We do not have to be theologians; we simply share the Christ of Scripture whom we find to be a reality in our own lives. Nor must we be professionally-trained preachers. The faith has always grown most effectively and rapidly where ordinary believers, living with the extraordinary Christ in their daily lives, have shared Him spontaneously and naturally with those around them.

The task of the apostles was to begin to share this Good News in ever-widening concentric circles. All that was lacking was power. The initiative and the power to witness would soon come when the Spirit of the risen Christ was poured out on His people.

Questions for Discussion

1. Have you ever thought about God's agenda for the church before? How does the agenda of your local congregation fit in with God's agenda as you understand it? How consistent are your personal priorities with God's priorities for His people?

2. Who are the "Samaritans" in your area? How can you and your church reach out to them?

3. If you were in the place of Jesus after the resurrection, how would you have used the 40 days before the ascension? How do you think Jesus used that time?

4. Can you share some specific way you have seen the Holy Spirit work recently? What is the greatest thing you have seen Him do?

5. Write down all the consequences of the resurrection you can think of.

6. Can you think of times when you have had as narrow a view of God's love as the disciples did? How can we overcome it?

7. What comes to your mind when you hear someone speak of Christian witness? Write down the basic elements you think should be included in your Christian witness. Share it with someone this week.

CHAPTER TWO

The Promise Fulfilled

Acts 2:1-41

A sense of need is one of God's greatest gifts. Until God gives us a deep sense of dissatisfaction with what we are in contrast to a vision of what He created us to be, we will never seek more of His purpose and power in our lives.

The apostles must have had an overwhelming sense of need. Can you imagine how they felt? They had lived with Jesus three years and had witnessed events no one had ever seen before. They had wondered at His teaching, marveled at His power as they experienced it in their own lives. They had watched Him heal the sick, liberate the demon-possessed and re-create lives shattered and broken by greed, lust and pride.

Then their dawning conviction that Jesus was indeed God's Messiah, the restorer of all things, was totally crushed. They watched Him as He was arrested, tried and killed like the worst of criminals. This had been followed by an event so earthshaking they could scarcely believe it, much less understand all its implications. Jesus had been raised from the dead! God had done something entirely new and unique. This event would change history and transform lives as no other before or since.

They had been witnesses of the pivotal event in human history! Now Jesus was gone, ascended to the seat of power. All they were charged to do was to go out and begin to convince a hostile, skeptical world of this incredible Good News, beginning in Jerusalem where He had been crucified! No wonder they joined together in constant prayer with His other followers, seeking and awaiting the promised gift of the Holy Spirit! They needed power beyond anything they had ever experienced before!

When God gives any of us a new, apparently impossible challenge in our lives, we have only two alternatives. The first is to run away, as Peter almost did after the resurrection saying, "I'm going fishing!" The other is to fall on our knees before God and trust Him to do His will in and through us, despite our inadequacies. Clearly, the apostles chose the second option.

Pentecost and the Old Testament Hope of the Spirit

Pentecost was one of the three major religious festivals of the Jewish year which all Jewish men living within 20 miles of Jerusalem were required to attend. The other two were Passover and the Feast of the Tabernacles. All three celebrated aspects of the Exodus, the establishment of the Covenant and the giving of the Promised Land. The festival was so named because it was celebrated 50 days after the first Sunday after Passover. Also called the "Feast of Weeks," its purposes were laid down in Leviticus 23; Numbers 28; and Deuteronomy 16. This was the day when the firstfruits of the wheat harvest were presented to God, thanking Him for giving His people the new land. As the celebration of the first fruits it pointed toward the greater gifts of God in the future. It also celebrated the anniversary of the giving of the Law at Sinai.

Now that the Jews were so widely scattered, it was impossible for most to attend all three feasts each year.

But an amazing number did come to Jerusalem to worship on these occasions. Because travel on the Mediterranean was safer in the late spring when Pentecost was celebrated, this festival normally brought the greatest multitudes to the city. Its normal population of fifty thousand ballooned to nearly one million at this time of year.

The Spirit of God was frequently mentioned in the Old Testament. But until Pentecost He was given only to special leaders of the people, primarily to prophets, and then only in crisis situations. He did not remain upon them. Moses longed for the time when the whole of God's people would be prophets and the Lord would give His Spirit to all (see Num. 11:29). Jeremiah envisioned the day of the New Covenant when the Law written on stone tablets would be replaced by the Law written in people's hearts (see Jer. 31:31-34). Isaiah told of the Messiah upon whom the Spirit would not be a sporadic gift but would remain (see 11:2) and Joel foresaw the time when God's Spirit would be poured out on all flesh (see Joel 2:28-32). These Old Testament promises were soon to be fulfilled as the infant church prayed on the day of Pentecost.

The Holy Spirit Is Poured Out

How does one attempt to describe the indescribable? The Holy Spirit, poured out on the people of God, came in wind and fire. These were marvelous symbols of His coming. In Hebrew and Greek the same word means both *wind* and *Spirit*. In his vision, when Ezekiel had called for wind to blow on dead bodies, it was the Spirit of God who came and filled them with life (see Ezek. 37:9-14). Jesus had compared the Spirit to the wind in His words to Nicodemus (see John 3:8). For the Spirit is like a wind, mighty, uncontrolable, seen only in His effects. Wind suggests incredible power, cleaning out something, bringing in the new. Fire too is a great symbol. It brings to mind awesome danger along with energy and purification. It suggests warmth, explosion, energy. John the Baptist predicted that the Messiah would baptize "with the Holy Spirit and with fire" (Luke 3:16).

Accompanying these outward phenomena of wind and fire, the Spirit came upon the whole body of believers with power and fullness that transcended any previous experience. Their praise went beyond the bounds of normal human speech. The Spirit of God came into their lives, began to dwell within them with power and intimacy never known before. The church, the new people of God, was born.

He came upon *all* believers, not just a few leaders. The Spirit was poured out on the whole fellowship and upon each individual within it. An entirely new phase of redemptive history began. The New Israel came to life. Henceforth it would be led and empowered by the Spirit as it began its mission of taking the gospel to the ends of the earth.

Consistent with Jesus' prediction in Acts 1:8, the primary effect of the Spirit's coming lay not in the inner experiences or the outward manifestations, but in the communication of the Good News. Still more striking was the universal scope of this communication.

The story of the tower of Babel in Genesis 11 told of the breakdown in communication and the scattering of the nations because of man's pride. The narrative of Abraham, starting in Genesis 12, unveiled the beginning of God's plan to reveal Himself to mankind and to bring men and women from all the families on earth into a new, blessed community. The outpouring of the Spirit at Pentecost, the result of the life, death and resurrection of Jesus Christ, was the reversal of Babel. The Spirit would reestablish communication between widely diverse peoples. It was the beginning of the fulfillment of the promise to Abraham that all the families of the earth would be blessed (see Gen. 12:3).

Communication Reestablished

Evidently by this time the believers were in the Temple precincts. Their loud praise soon brought a crowd of devout Jews from other parts of the Temple. They came from many nations and represented in embryo the whole world.

There were people from all the far-flung lands where Jews of the diaspora lived: from Mesopotamia and other areas to the east, Asia Minor to the northwest, Egypt and Libya to the southwest, Arabia directly south, from Crete and further west from Rome itself. Both those who had been born Jews and those who had adopted the faith were present, now coming to hear the apostles.

The most remarkable phenomenon at Pentecost was yet to come. Every one in this diverse group would hear the mighty works of God told in his own language! This is puzzling! All those present undoubtedly understood Aramaic or Greek or both. The apostles spoke both languages. Why was it necessary for every man to hear in his own native tongue? Wouldn't it have been enough for Peter and the others to have spoken one of these two well-known languages?

There are two reasons for this miracle. First, even though one may speak two or more languages, the deepest communication to the heart, at the most personal level, takes place in the language he learned at his mother's knee. There are many examples of this in mission history. Even though many of the Chol Indians of southern Mexico understood the Spanish into which the Bible had been translated, few of them had become believers. But since the Scriptures have been translated into Chol and they realize that God "spoke their own language," the church has grown rapidly among them.

Secondly, this event was a powerful symbol pointing to the day when, under the guidance of the same Holy Spirit, people of every race and tongue would hear the Good News in their own language, believe and become a part of the Body of Christ. Thus the miracle of Pentecost is the beginning of the fulfillment of Acts 1:8 and points to its final goal.

It is important to note the focus of the message heard by this diverse group of Jews. The disciples of Jesus did not talk of their marvelous experience; rather they spoke of the mighty works of God. Those works will always be the primary focus of the work of the Spirit and of genuine Christian witness. Peter makes this clear in the first Christian sermon.

The Mighty Works of God

The account of Peter's sermon is an excellent summary both of his message on this occasion and of the fundamental proclamation of the message of the early church. We see it repeated several times in Acts and discover it in the New Testament letters as well. Make no mistake about it—the Christian message is clear and consistent. It always begins with the mighty and unique acts of God in history, explains their meaning for us and invites our response. Thus it is news, not advice, incredible good news for all who believe! When I was a young, inexperienced missionary in Mato Grosso, on Brazil's western frontier, I wanted to be sure the message I shared was authentic and biblical. So I frequently turned to Acts and examined the basic message of the early church. We can do no better than to model our preaching and witness on this basic message.

Peter begins, probably with good humor, by answering those who accused the believers of being drunk. He quickly moves to the heart of the matter. What the believers had experienced and the others had seen was not the result of wine; it was the gift of God's Holy Spirit. This was not an aberration; it was part and parcel of the redemptive history recorded in the Old Testament which they were there to celebrate. We should remember that Peter's hearers were all Jews, devout enough to make the long journey to Jerusalem. Nurtured on the Old Testament, they were there to celebrate God's redemption in the past, at the same time hoping He would act again in the future.

Now, Peter said, that very day God had fulfilled the promise made through the prophet Joel centuries earlier. In these last days He had poured out His Spirit on all flesh. Now the Spirit was given, not just to a few selected leaders and not only in crisis. He was now God's gift to all believers, young and old, male and female, slave and free. Along with this gift to God's people, salvation would be taken to all the earth. But this had come about only because a far greater promise had been fulfilled, the one they all awaited. It was this remarkable Good News that Peter now proclaimed.

Jesus Christ was the subject of this basic Christian message. No Christian, no church has anything authentic to say if it does not begin with Him and base all it says on His life, death, resurrection and ministry. Jesus of Nazareth, accredited by God, had done mighty works among them. Even the strangers in the crowd had heard of them and many at least had recognized they could have been done only by divine power. The miracles of Jesus were not mere wonders; they were "signs" of the Kingdom of God, signs that God had come to His people. Indeed, as Peter pointed out, it was God Himself who had performed these mighty works through Jesus.

Yet the Jews, led by their priests, had engineered

His condemnation and handed Jesus over to pagan rulers to be crucified. But even though they were guilty of His death, they had unconsciously fulfilled the purpose of God. He had revealed through His prophets that the Messiah should suffer and die for the sins of many.

Now Peter came to the heart of his message, the point to which he devoted the most attention. God had raised Jesus from the dead! Given who He was and what God had sent Him to do, it was simply unthinkable that death should have held Him. It would have implied that sin, evil and death had defeated God Himself! Just as the Messiah's death had been ordained by God, so was His resurrection and glory. The Jewish council had condemned Jesus as an imposter and blasphemer. God had reversed the verdict of the council and put the stamp of approval on all that Jesus had said and done by raising Him from the dead!

Jewish tradition said that the truth should be established by at least two witnesses. Now Peter called first on the witness of the Old Testament Scriptures which they all acknowledged. He quoted Psalm 16:10 where David had written: "You will not abandon me to the grave, nor will you let your Holy One see decay." The psalmist could not have been speaking of himself, Peter said. They all knew he had died and gone to his grave. His tomb could be visited near the city. Rather, inspired by the Spirit of God, David had spoken of the coming Messiah, whom the King himself prefigured.

Then Peter made the most startling claim of all. He boldly declared that he and the other apostles standing with him were eyewitnesses of the resurrection. They had seen Him, talked with and been with Him for 40 days. We recall that when it came time to choose a successor of Judas in the apostolic band, the requirement was clear. It was necessary that the man had been with

Jesus and the others from the baptism of John until the
ascension in order that he too might be a witness of the
resurrection. This was the foundation stone of the
Good News, and to be an apostle was to be sent out as
a witness of that event.

After proclaiming that Jesus had risen, Peter
answered the question as to where Jesus was now.
Echoing both the words of Jesus before the high priest
(see Luke 22:69) and the last line of Psalm 16 which he
had just quoted, he said the Messiah was now at the
right hand of God, in the seat of authority. Having
received the promised Holy Spirit from the Father, He
had now poured Him out on His followers. Thus the victory of Jesus was not only indicated by Old Testament
prophecy and by the apostles; it had been shown by the
gift of the Spirit. Peter's listeners could first of all see
the outward manifestations of this event; now he had
explained its meaning. Soon they would be invited to
become participants themselves.

Peter concluded his message with a ringing but
awesome declaration, "God has made this Jesus, whom
you crucified, both Lord and Christ" (Acts 2:36). We
are so accustomed to using these terms, sometimes
glibly, that we may miss their impact, especially on that
group of devout Jews. First, there was the contrast
between God's evaluation of Jesus and theirs. The Jewish council, supposedly the guardian of religious tradition and purity, had rejected and condemned Him to
death. God had reversed that judgment and vindicated
Jesus by raising Him from the dead. He was the Messiah (Christ in Greek) or Anointed One, the unique
descendent of David, whom they had long awaited.

There was an even greater surprise in Peter's declaration. He proclaimed that Jesus was Lord! This was a
more inclusive term than Christ, both for the native
Jewish hearers and for proselytes of pagan background.

It was an amazing, even shocking, affirmation. When the Old Testament was translated into Greek, the term Lord (*Kurios* in Greek) had been used for *Yahweh*, the name of the God of Israel. Thus in declaring Jesus to be Lord, Peter clearly identified this crucified and resurrected Messiah with the one true God Himself.

For listeners of Greek as well as those of Jewish background Peter's words affirmed Jesus to be the ultimate authority within history and beyond, above that of any religious tradition or political state, above that of the rabbis or Caesar. Jesus' authority was that of God Himself. The first Christian creed would be "Jesus is Lord," and an early hymn in Philippians 2:6-11, would look toward the day when every tongue would confess that Jesus indeed is Lord.

The Cry for Help and the Good News

Martin Luther often said we must hear the bad news before we can hear the Good News. Peter's message, if true, must have appeared to be the worst possible news to the crowd. They and their leaders had not only rejected the long-awaited Messiah; they had put themselves clearly in opposition to God by crucifying Him! Was it any wonder they were cut to the heart and cried for help!

Peter's message is a marvelous example of the preaching of the cross. His hearers realized as never before the depth of sin and its effects. It was both collective and individual, national and personal. Not only had their leaders rejected the Messiah and been responsible for His murder; they too had been personally involved and were responsible. Some who were there had no doubt been part of the mob which had shouted, "Crucify Him! Crucify Him!" Now they felt desperate.

Peter answered their cry with the amazing Good

News. They were not lost; they were not irrevocably rejected by God. Through repentance and faith in this crucified Messiah they would receive two gifts greater than any they had ever hoped for.

The first was the forgiveness of their sins. The greatest of their sins was of course complicity in the death of Jesus. It was an indication of the greatness of God's power and love that He could take that seemingly tragic event and make it the means of redemption even for murderers of His Son. With that would come forgiveness of all other sin. This was the fundamental gift offered by Christ. It was not the only gift of the gospel, but it was the one that unlocked and opened the door to all the others.

The second gift promised by Peter was the Holy Spirit. The fulfillment of Joel's prophecy would continue. Just as forgiveness would be given to all who repented and believed, so the Holy Spirit would be poured out to dwell permanently within them.

The risen Jesus would bestow both gifts on His people, the gift of the Spirit as well as the gift of forgiveness. The Spirit would be the Spirit of Jesus. He would lead them further in their understanding of His own truth. The Spirit would empower them both to live new lives and to continue the ministry and mission of the risen Lord out into the world.

However, these gifts would come only with repentance and baptism. *Repentance* was a term often used by John the Baptist and Jesus. It simply meant "to change one's mind" or "to turn around." They were to change their minds about Jesus and recognize Him as Messiah and Lord of their lives. They were to change their minds about their values, their priorities and goals in life as they sought to understand and adopt the new goals and values given by Jesus. They also were to change their minds about their sins, turning away from them to follow the Lord Jesus Christ.

Baptism with water had been used by John the Baptist to symbolize repentance and a new beginning. After the resurrection Jesus had commanded His followers to make disciples of all nations and to baptize them in the name of the Father, Son and Holy Spirit (see Matt. 28:19). Now it was time to begin. Baptism would be the outward sign of one's union with Christ through repentance and faith, his reception of the Holy Spirit and his commitment to be the Lord's.

Peter's sermon at Pentecost is an excellent example of the message of the early church which scholars call the *kerygma*, or proclamation. We notice the same basic elements in other sermons in Acts (e.g. Acts 13:17-39) and the same framework in the Gospels. The primary points are:

1. The Old Testament promises are now fulfilled; the new age has arrived.

2. God has brought this about through the life, death and resurrection of Jesus the Messiah. Even His death came about through the plan of God, and His resurrection was God's stamp of approval on all of His life and ministry.

3. God has exalted Jesus to His right hand; He is now Lord over all.

4. In Christ God offers forgiveness of sins to all who repent and believe.

It was clear that this was news, not mere advice, the kind of news that demanded a response, a yes or a no!

The Invitation Is to All

Even now we hear the universal note which is so prevalent in Acts. Jesus' words in Acts 1:8 are echoed as Peter assured them that the promise is not only for them and their children, but "for all who are far off—for all whom the Lord our God will call" (Acts 2:39). Those who were "far off" would some day include a multitude of people from many more diverse groups than Peter and his companions ever dreamed of!

But note the varying response of the crowd. Some, witnessing one of the most crucial events in history, simply shrugged it off with the words, "They are drunk!" Others, drawn by the noise, remained to listen to this first proclamation of the gospel. No doubt some of them rejected Peter's words. Perhaps they could not get beyond their prejudices against a message which came through "unofficial" channels. Perhaps they could not deal with the awfulness of their sin revealed by the apostle's sermon and consequently denied its validity. Whatever the reasons, these people would judge themselves by the way in which they responded to the Good News.

But the greatest manifestation of the power of the Holy Spirit on this occasion was now seen. The Spirit, using the words of Peter, broke through the barriers of tradition, indifference and hostility, leading three thousand people to repent and believe in the crucified and risen Messiah as their Lord. As Jesus had promised, the Spirit had come. As a result witness was given powerfully in the first circle, Jerusalem; and the church, the Body of Christ, was born.

Questions for Discussion

1. Have you ever been faced with an apparently impossible task, as the disciples were? What did you do? What can we learn from them in this event?

2. What aspect of the coming of the Spirit on the day of Pentecost impresses you most? Why? What have you learned from it?

3. Go over Peter's message and write down the main parts as you understand them. Does your under-

standing of the gospel line up with them? Could you explain the gospel clearly to someone else?

4. What do you mean when you say Jesus is Lord? What does this mean for history? For your life?

5. Write down everything you think Peter meant when he said, "Repent!" What does repentance mean in your life?

CHAPTER THREE

The New People of God

Acts 2:42—4:37

From the very beginning, God's strategy of redemption was to form a new and special people with a unique mission in history. We see this in the story of Abraham when God promised to give him an heir and make him a great nation. The purpose of this was not simply to reward Abraham for his faith, nor was the nation to be an end in itself. The primary purpose of God's call to Abraham was that through him and his descendents all the "peoples on earth [would] be blessed" (Gen. 12:3).

When the Covenant made with Abraham was renewed and deepened at Sinai, the people were told they would be "a kingdom of priests and a holy nation" (Exod. 19:6). Even though they understood few if any of the implications of this statement, God's plan was becoming more clear. A priest was one who served as a mediator between God and man, speaking to God on behalf of the people and to the people on behalf of God. The root meaning of *holy* was not ethically pure as we use the word today. Rather the word indicated that they were to be different, set apart for a special purpose, and therefore pure.

God's purpose was to use this unique nation as a vehicle of His revelation to all the nations in order that all might know and serve Him. This became more explicit in the book of Isaiah. The prophet spoke of the day when the earth would "be full of the knowledge of the Lord as the waters cover the sea" (11:9). God would make the Servant of the Lord, identified with the true Israel, "a covenant for the people and a light for the Gentiles" (42:6). The offerings of foreigners would be acceptable in Jerusalem and the Lord's house would be called "a house of prayer for all nations" (56:7).

The tragedy of the Jewish nation was that it had attempted to cling to the blessings of God while rejecting His purpose—the mission to which He had called them. Their rabbinical tradition was admirable in many respects as it led them to attempt to fulfill every aspect of the Law. But an increasingly defensive mentality, coupled with pride in their past, led some Jews to look on all Gentiles (i.e. non-Jews) as fit only for the flames of hell. At best they believed that the Gentiles were destined to become their servants. One aspect of Jesus' ministry which most infuriated the religious leaders was that He showed God's acceptance of all who had faith, Jew or non-Jew, keeper of the Law or not.

Thus for first-century Jews, their understanding of themselves as a special people focused far more on privilege than on responsibility. It was narrowly defined in terms of keeping the Law, with circumcision essential. And while Judaism engaged in some proselytism, its attitude toward non-Jews was almost entirely negative. They were thought to be outside the pale of God's love and purpose. The Old Testament promise that the Jews would be a light to the Gentiles was largely forgotten or rejected.

God's New People

Jesus understood that He came not only to die and rise again for our sins, but to form the new people of God, the new Israel. His selection of 12 men to accompany Him as disciples constituted a walking parable. Just as the old Israel had begun with 12 patriarchs, so would the new. A part of the appeal of Peter's sermon at Pentecost was for the people to separate themselves from the old corrupt Israel and form the new. Years later, in words reminiscent of Exodus 19:6, he would tell the church they were "a chosen people, a royal priesthood, a holy nation, a people belonging to God, that [they] may declare the praises of him who called [them] out of darkness into his wonderful light" (1 Pet. 2:9).

Jesus did not come to save disembodied souls or merely to form a conglomeration of redeemed individuals, each primarily concerned with his own salvation and needs. He came to form a new humanity whose pattern of life is shown here. These early believers were not perfect any more than we are. But they knew God had called them to be new people and they knew the vibrating, pulsating power of God's Spirit within their lives and within this new community.

Just as the Spirit was given as the firstfruits of the completely redeemed life, so the New Israel was to be a showcase of the new humanity! Even with all its failures it was to point toward God's ultimate plan for His redeemed creation.

Membership in the new people of God would not be determined by race or culture. Even though all of those in this first church were born Jews or were proselytes, the criterion for entrance was now different. There were two ways one could become a member of the old Israel: (1) he was born into it or (2) he entered it by adopting a certain set of beliefs and a specific culture. Jewish faith and culture were inseparable. You could not be fully accepted as a member of the religious group without accepting its culture and life-style.

Since all believers at this point were Jews, the distinction between their faith and culture was not yet clear. They still thought of themselves as practicing Jews. The difference was that they also worshiped Jesus as the crucified and resurrected Messiah. Some no doubt hoped the entire nation would soon share their faith in Him.

However the center of their faith, the basis of their new community and the criteria for entrance into it had shifted radically. The question was not whether one was strict in keeping the Law as with groups like the Pharisees and Essenes. The only question was that of repentance and faith in Jesus as Lord and Christ, publicly professed by baptism, followed by entrance into the infant church. None of the apostles or other believers yet realized the full implication of these new criteria. But the Spirit was gradually opening new doors. The essence of the Good News was that everyone, not just a spiritual, cultural or racial elite, was invited to repent, believe and become part of the new people of God.

The New Life-Style—Model for Today

Nearly two thousand years of history have passed since Pentecost. There have been many examples of courage and faithfulness during that period. But often the centuries have caused congregations to forget the apostolic message, to distort the distinctive life-style of the first disciples, to ignore the mission our Lord gave to His followers and to become just another institution plagued by the humdrum and routine.

Thus all of us are seeking in one way or another to encourage a renewal of the life of the Spirit and the mission of Christ in the churches of which we are a part. The first Christian community, the early church, will serve as the model in our quest. Here we discover the essential characteristics of the church. Here we see that ordinary people responsive to the Spirit make an enormous impact on their city and world. We are seized with the conviction and hope that God will do it again, if we His people are responsive.

If this first church is a prescription for the church in every era, we would do well to go back and reexamine it. As the saying goes, When all else fails, read the directions!

We do well to remember that the basis of the new community was the conviction that Jesus was not only the Messiah; He was Lord! He was the ultimate authority for each believer. Often in the evangelical church we have stressed Jesus as Saviour without putting equal stress on His Lordship. He can be Saviour only if He is the Lord over sin and death and Lord over history. We cannot accept Him as Saviour without following Him also as our Lord. To know Jesus as Lord means to make His will for our personal lives, for His church and for His world our highest priority.

The Apostles' Teaching

The first believers in the young church were eager to know their Lord better. They had a magnificent resource available. The apostles, who had accompanied Jesus during the three years of His public ministry from His baptism to His resurrection, were there. Is it any wonder that the first characteristic we see is that "they devoted themselves to the apostles' teaching" (Acts 2:42)? The phrase means they persisted in listening to that teaching. Over and over again the Twelve would recount to rapt groups of inquirers and believers the events of Jesus' life. As they told of miracles of healing, no doubt some of those who had been healed, like the man from the pool of Bethesda, were there to add their witness. As they told of total acceptance and forgiveness for the most unlikely sinners, those who had experienced it from Jesus must have added their confirmation.

However, the apostles' instruction went beyond the events of Jesus' life to His teaching. This was more than a new set of moral maxims; it involved a reordering of life's priorities. One's goal was no longer to get as much as possible for himself; it was to serve and glorify God. It brought a new way of looking at one's neighbor, even of defining who was the neighbor. He was no longer an object of indifference, or even an enemy; he was one whom God loved, for whom Christ had died, one with whom to share the Good News. Leadership and privilege were not to be used to dominate others; they were to be used to serve, even as Christ had served.

This remarkable new teaching was not an empty ideal suitable only for the hopelessly naive. It was grounded in the reality of God's loving, powerful action in Christ. Because He had committed Himself to His people in the cross and resurrection, they could trust Him completely with their lives and their possessions. It would take centuries, all of human history, for the church to plumb all the depths of Jesus' teaching and begin to understand all its implications. But the early church eagerly began; and we must continue.

We do not have the apostles with us. But we have their record of Jesus' life and teaching. We have the Old Testament which tells of God's mighty acts for His people long before Christ came. These point to the Saviour. We have the New Testament letters in which the apostles dealt with specific problems in young churches and explored further the implications of the gospel. In the Old and New Testaments, inspired by the same Holy Spirit present in the early church, we have an even greater resource than did those first believers. The Scriptures are now complete. And for us as for the first believers, one essential sign of a vital church is that we want to know Christ so well that we devote ourselves to the apostles' teaching.

Fellowship

Secondly, they devoted themselves to fellowship. The Greek word here, *koinonia*, is well-known. But it means more than most of us understand or practice. It is a deep sharing of common life. The early church recognized that they belonged to each other because they belonged to the same Lord who had ransomed them. They had all received the same Spirit. Paul would later describe it, "We were all baptized by one Spirit into one body . . . and we were all given the one Spirit to drink" (1 Cor. 12:13). They had the same basic human needs. They needed the forgiveness, grace and power of God in their personal lives. They needed the support and care of each other. And they recognized that these two could not be separated. The gifts of God more often than not came to them through their new-found brethren. The encouragement and help they received in the *koinonia* were among the greatest of God's gifts to them.

One other factor drew them close together and was a clear indication of the presence of the Holy Spirit: Together they were committed to the mission of Christ, to live and witness in such a manner that He would become known and served throughout their city and beyond. I once read of a marine sergeant who, although wounded, left the hospital to rejoin his comrades in heavy combat, almost losing his life in the process. As he later analyzed why he had done it, he realized it was the oneness he felt with the others in a common cause. He simply had to be with them because they were called together to the same task. The Spirit calls every believer to take part in the mission of

Christ. In doing so we experience the deepest sense of *koinonia*.

Worship

Thirdly, the believers devoted themselves to the breaking of bread and to prayer, that is to worship in its various forms. It is clear that they continued to attend public worship in the Temple. There was no reason not to; they had not ceased to be Jews. They were the true Israel, followers of the Messiah. They no doubt went to the Temple both to show their continuity with ancient Israel and to bear witness to the risen Christ. But the more formal and traditional worship in the Temple was not enough. That worship celebrated the mighty acts of God in centuries past. The worship of the New Israel unquestionably must have focused on the greatest of all of God's acts, the one which the Temple worship hoped for and anticipated, the coming of Christ.

Because the worship of the church centered on the fulfillment of all the hopes and promises of the past in Jesus Christ it was necessary for the believers to worship as a separate community. We wish Luke had told us more about the forms of their worship. But we can see that it must have included at least four elements: (1) the teaching of the apostles, which we have already mentioned; (2) prayer; (3) praise; and (4) the breaking of bread.

Prayer included the formal liturgical prayers and psalms of Temple worship and probably some of the prayers of the synagogue, now adapted for Christian worship. The believers must have learned and used together the prayer Jesus taught His disciples. No doubt it also included free, spontaneous intercession and praise, concerned at times with specific needs but focused primarily on their desire to be faithful witnesses no matter what obstacles they faced. The prayer of Peter and John after they had been threatened by the Jewish council is an excellent example (see Acts 4:23-30).

So it was with praise. There was formal praise, often using the psalms in the Temple, and both formal and informal praise in the separate Christian worship. Praise in this Spirit-filled Body was constant, praise to God for His mighty works in the past, for the healings and wonders being performed among them and above all for Jesus Christ in whom all the gifts of God came together.

They broke bread together, not in the Temple area but in private homes. It was an expression of several facets of their life together. The term first of all makes us think of Jesus feeding the five thousand (see Luke 9:16), eating with His disciples before the crucifixion (see Luke 22:19), and of His post-resurrection appearances (see Luke 24:30; John 21:13). Thus it must have been an act of worship, a sacramental meal which celebrated His death, resurrection and coming Kingdom as well as His continued presence.

This act of worship around the table of the Lord was apparently also a very practical way of expressing *koinonia*. Those who had houses and food shared with those who did not. They were already practicing the gift of hospitality (see Rom. 12:13).

But whatever the forms or places, worship was clearly central in the church. It included proclamation and celebration of the mighty acts of God, focusing above all on Jesus Christ. It rejoiced in the promise of His return and praised Him for all of His gifts. It included prayer for His speedy return, for faithfulness in witness and for every kind of need. It also included a simple fellowship meal where Christ's presence was recognized, His cross and resurrection celebrated and where those in need were cared for.

We can imagine the excitement and power that swirled around the new community. The risen Christ healed men and women of all sorts of diseases as He had in the past. But now He did it through the apostles. Believers and nonbelievers alike were filled with a sense of awe at such clear indications of God's power and presence. The sense of *koinonia*, or oneness in the church, had led those who had more to share with those who had less. Many sold what they had in order to do so. No one had ever seen a group like this one. It was the complete opposite of religious groups which drew themselves apart, excluded most people and despised outsiders. These followers of Jesus accepted all who came and confessed Him as Lord; and they shared with them whatever their need. Is it any wonder they found favor with the people and grew rapidly?

Two Illustrations

After this thumbnail sketch of the early church in Acts 2:42-47, Luke gives us two marvelous illustrations of the spirit and power of the group.

The first is the healing of the lame man at the Temple gate. Imagine the contrast! The most beautiful gate of the magnificent Temple built by Herod the Great. The gate, made of Corinthian bronze, had sculpted on it a vine, one of the Old Testament symbols of Israel, indicating that she was to bear fruit for God (see Luke 20:9-16). Just as tourists find in poorer countries that beggars sit at the entrance to churches and temples in hope that people will be more generous there, so it was with this man. Crippled from birth, dressed in rags, he begged every day at this gate.

Most people on seeing a beggar, hurry by as quickly as possible, whether or not they throw him some coins on the way. This man must have been surprised when the disciples gazed at him and told him to look at them.

Then his high expectations gave way to despair at Peter's words, "Silver or gold I do not have," only to become delight and astonishment at the following words, "In the name of Jesus Christ of Nazareth, walk" (Acts 3:6)! Through Christ, Peter and John had given the beggar not alms to continue his miserable existence but an entirely new life, physically, spiritually and socially. He no doubt took his place among the followers of Jesus. He was an example of the total healing Christ had brought.

Naturally the man's praises could not be contained and a crowd came running. When they learned what had happened they shared the beggar's amazement. Peter immediately began to speak to them. First he disclaimed any special power or godliness and made it clear that Jesus was the healer. As a Jew speaking to Jews he was careful to link Jesus with their God, the God of Abraham, Isaac and Jacob. They had come to the Temple to worship the God of their fathers, the God of the Exodus, of David, of the prophets. Why should they think it strange, Peter asked them, that God should continue to do mighty works? God was not dead, not a musty myth of the past; He was alive! Peter's message now was similar to that of the day of Pentecost.

But we wonder if Peter, as he pondered both the Old Testament and the words of Jesus, was beginning to see the larger dimensions of God's plan for all peoples. Just before he was cut off by the Temple guards he quoted Genesis 22:18, "Through your offspring all peoples on earth will be blessed" (Acts 3:25). Then he added that God had sent Jesus His servant *first* to the Jews to bless them, implying that His purpose was to include others as well.

At any rate the Jewish leaders could not tolerate such preaching. Alarmed at the growth of this new sect, fearful that it would undermine their own power and privilege, they were determined to put an end to the matter and expected to do so by intimidating the apostles.

The scene the next day would have been humorous if not so serious. Two relatively unlettered fishermen, "blue-collar types," faced the religious, intellectual and economic elite of Judea. It is hard to believe that one of the two had run away a few weeks earlier when this same group had manipulated the Roman governor into condemning Jesus. Do we need any greater indication of the power of the Holy Spirit?

The irony here lay in the fact that the religious leaders, whom Peter and John faced, were the conservators of the Jewish traditions. The Law, the Temple and its ritual were all intended to lead the people to worship and celebrate the God who had done mighty acts of liberation in the past. But they did not believe He would do anything in the present! Nor did they want Him to!

The power of the apostles, on the other hand, came from their conviction that the same God was still at work, that He had done His greatest deed of all in Jesus Christ, and that He continued to act through His Spirit in the present. They had seen it, they had experienced it in that very moment of crisis! That was the source of their courage and confidence. This conviction of God's sovereignty and continued activity led them to defy the rulers quietly but firmly, then to pray not for protection but for boldness.

One of the most rapidly growing denominations in the world is the Assembly of God in Brazil. Begun in 1911, it had grown to 5.6 million believers by 1980. A study of that church indicated that its most outstanding characteristic was the expectation that God would work here and now in the lives of His people. There are other important characteristics, of course, some of which other Christians might criticize. But its spectacular growth indicates that people are not seeking a memorial to a far-off God, a remote Christ; they are seeking a community of believers who know He is alive and experience His power in the present.

Luke's second illustration of the life-style of the early church was Joseph, also called Barnabas, a Hellenistic Jewish believer from Cyprus, one of the most attractive people in the entire Bible. We also will meet him at crucial points later on. He was one of those who sold his property and gave the money to the apostles for them to use for those in need. We should not think this was required in the early church. Other passages show that it was voluntary; there were those who kept their property. How else could the church have worshiped in various homes?

But generosity was not the greatest of Joseph's qualities. His nickname, "Barnabas," shows that. The Greek word is *parakleseos*, which comes from the same root as *paraclete*, the word Jesus used to describe the Holy Spirit in John 14:26 and 16:7. It means "one called to stand alongside." The term has been translated in many ways: advocate, helper, comforter (one who makes the other strong), counselor and encourager. We could add to the list.

Barnabas was a man so filled with the Holy Spirit that his ministry in the lives of others was like that of the Spirit Himself. He embodied genuine *koinonia* in his life. Whatever the need of another believer was, Barnabas stood alongside him, helping with his needs, affirming him as a child of God, encouraging him in his Christian faith and service. Barnabas stands as a model for every Christian as he stands alongside his brothers and sisters in the Body of Christ.

The church was alive and growing. It was not made up of perfect people. They all had much to learn. They would soon face strife and terrible persecution. But God was forging it into His instrument of witness within Jerusalem, to Judea and beyond. More barriers would soon be broken by the gospel.

Questions for Discussion

1. If a non-Christian friend asked what the purpose of your church was, how would you respond? What could you learn about its purpose from Acts 1 and 2?

2. How is the lordship of Christ taught and expressed in your church?

3. Compare the life-style of your congregation with that of the early church.

    a. In what ways do you devote yourselves to the apostles' teaching?

    b. How does fellowship (*koinonia*) develop, especially among newcomers? Write down some ways in which it is expressed.

    c. What do you understand worship to be? Have you ever attempted to define it (see Rom. 12:1,2)?

4. Have you ever known someone who deserved to be called a Barnabas? What steps do you wish to take in your life toward becoming an "alongside person"?

CHAPTER FOUR

Persecution and Apparent Tragedy

Acts 6:1—8:4

A dramatic, history-changing new phase in the life of the church was about to begin. It was triggered when some of the widows complained they were being short-changed in the daily food distribution. Because of this incident, chapter 6 marks a new division in Acts. Soon the church would be moved beyond the first circle by unexpected and apparently tragic circumstances.

The early church was vital and Spirit-filled, but not perfect! It had grown to include perhaps 15 thousand people, many of whom were poor. A number of them were widows who depended on the charity of the Christian community. The apostles were in danger of becoming swamped by the administration of the resources necessary for their communal life.

The situation was complicated by the existence of two groups in the church—the Aramaic-speaking community or *Hebrews*, and the Greek speakers or *Hellenists*. Both groups were Jewish Christians. Those born and raised in Palestine spoke Aramaic, a linguistic sister of Hebrew which by now had died out in daily life. The Hellenists had been born and raised in foreign countries and Greek was their language. In some cases their families had lived outside Palestine for centuries. They were of course more integrated into the Gentile world and somewhat more open to association with non-Jews.

Palestinian Jews, rigidly orthodox, hated all things Gentile and prided themselves in being uncontaminated by tolerance of anything pagan. Thus they often looked down on the Hellenistic Jews, believing them to be spiritually inferior. Some of the tension between the two groups survived even in the church and the widows among the Greek-speaking believers complained, whether justifiably or not, that they were suffering discrimination.

There was another danger threatening the Christian community. By now three to five years old it had not moved beyond Jerusalem. Perhaps the rapid growth of the church in the city led the apostles to feel they could not spare anyone to go beyond. Perhaps they believed they should concentrate all their witness at the center of the nation's life. For even some of the priests had become believers. At any rate the new Israel had already settled down in Jerusalem, awaiting the Lord's return, hoping to bring the rest of the nation to faith in Christ. But it was in terrible danger of forgetting her Lord's command to go to the rest of the world.

The Election of the Seven: Stephen

The apostles wisely realized they needed additional leadership in administering the church. Otherwise they would be diverted from their primary task of giving firsthand witness to the life, death and resurrection of Jesus. The whole congregation, showing remarkable sensitivity, chose seven men, apparently all of whom, according to their names, were Hellenists. Men from the group which believed it suffered discrimination were put in charge of the daily distribution.

Stephen comes to center stage at this point as one of those chosen to administer the food. Outstanding in every way, he is a remarkable example of what it means to be God's person, no matter how difficult the circumstances. He also stands as one of the greatest illustrations of God's sovereign power to turn apparent tragedy and defeat into triumph. Many do not realize that, in addition, he broke new theological ground in his understanding of the gospel. He saw more clearly than others that God was not limited to one place or people. His ministry in life and death would open the door to the realization of the universal dimension of the gospel.

Luke tells us three times that Stephen was full of the Holy Spirit, adding also that he was full of faith, wisdom, grace and power. Obviously brilliant, deeply versed in Scripture and a powerful speaker, this man was destined to play an important role in the life and witness of the church.

It is all the more striking that the first job Stephen accepted was the sometimes tedious, often thankless task of administering the daily dole. It was not a position that appeared to be very prestigious or "spiritual." Yet one sure sign of the fullness of the Spirit is willingness to accept the servant role, even as Christ did. Many are unwilling to accept a humble task, feeling it to be unworthy of them. But Stephen sought no glory or recognition for himself, only the privilege of serving as God led him.

Faith, another characteristic of Stephen, was more than belief in Jesus as Messiah and Lord. It meant that he realized that Christ, the source of all life and power, was absolutely trustworthy. This was the kind of faith that came as he continued to take new steps in discipleship, discovering in the process that Christ was worthy of complete confidence. His wisdom was seen in his deep understanding of the Old Testament Scriptures and their fulfillment in Jesus. This gave him a perspective on history that would deeply challenge and disturb his antagonists, who could not accept its implications. As Stephen's ministry extended beyond administration to teaching and preaching the power of God became evident through him. Like the apostles, he performed wonders and signs which pointed beyond the acts themselves to the risen Lord, and in all this the grace of God made him almost universally winsome.

These gifts made Stephen a powerful advocate of the gospel in the synagogue where most of the Hellenists worshiped. Among those who attended were Jews from Cilicia, whose major city was Tarsus. Thus Saul, the zealous young Pharisee from that city, must have heard Stephen's message and realized very quickly what a strong challenge it posed to his deeply-held beliefs. These two adversaries saw much more clearly than others that the gospel of Christ was completely different from the message of Judaism. The latter promised acceptance by God to those who kept every detail of the Law. The new message offered grace and forgiveness to all who simply repented and believed in Christ. The two theologies could not coexist within the framework of Judaism. The old tradition would have to destroy the new "sect," or see itself undermined by its radically different message. Jesus had warned that the old wineskins could not contain the new wine. Up to now the church and Judaism had existed together, although not without tension. But the time had come when the old wineskins would burst!

Stephen's Trial and Defense

More of Stephen's adversaries began to see the far-reaching implications of his message and tried unsuccessfully to answer him. Then they attempted a different strategy. They accused him of speaking against the two most sacred aspects of Jewish religion, the Temple and the Law. To the Jew, the Temple was the only place where sacrifices could be offered and God truly worshiped. It was also the source of livelihood for most of Jerusalem, directly or indirectly. Thus the charge of speaking against the Temple was calculated to infuriate all the people of the city. The Law, as subsequent history after the destruction of the Temple would show, was even more essential in defining and preserving Judaism. Given through Moses but little observed during the centuries up to the fall of Jerusalem, it had become the essential mark of a Jew during and after the exile. Indeed without the strong emphasis on the Law, it is probable that the Jews would not have survived as a separate people, especially outside Palestine. Thus an attack on the Law would seem to be an attack on the very identity of the Jews.

Stephen learned Jesus' teachings well from the apostles. The accusation against him, almost identical to that against Jesus (see Mark 14:57-59), was a distortion of his teaching but not without some truth. Jesus had said, "Destroy this temple, and I will raise it again in three days" (John 2:19). Our Lord spoke, of course, of His resurrection. Probably He referred to the New Temple, the church, as well. Stephen must have quoted this saying more than once. He probably cited Jesus' words to the Samaritan woman—that true worship of God was a matter of the heart, not location (see John 4:21-24). Jesus' praise of the faith of the Roman centurion (see Luke 7:9) and His words about the true children of Abraham (John 8:31-47) were possibly quoted by Stephen.

Thus Stephen began to grasp the inner meaning of Jesus' teaching—the contrast between the provisional nature of the Temple and the Law, and the permanent nature of God's offer in Christ. While most followers of Christ continued to attend Temple services and were still seen as devout Jews, Stephen began to realize that the work of Christ superceded both Temple and Law. The gospel meant the end of the sacrificial system and of the Law as a means of justification. This in turn would mean the end of Jewish exclusiveness and would open the Kingdom to all who had faith in the Messiah.

History and theology were never separate in the Old Testament. The Scriptures told the history of God's dealing with His people, adding the meaning of that history, and the lessons drawn from it by the prophets under the inspiration of the Holy Spirit. One great similarity between the prophets and the apostles was that both knew God was still active in the present. Their adversaries, on the other hand, seemed to believe that God, who had done mighty acts in the past, was no longer active.

Stephen stood squarely in the tradition of the prophets and apostles in his interpretation both of the Old Testament and recent events. But he seems to have seen the implications of them more clearly than even the apostles did at this point.

The Defense

The amount of space Luke devoted to Stephen's address—over twice as much as to any other in Acts—is an indication that he saw it as a pivotal event in the history of the early church. The speech was not a defense of Stephen himself; it was a defense of the gospel he preached.

Stephen presented a theology of history which put the sovereign, saving action of God in the center. He began and ended his address by stressing that God's power and presence were not limited to one particular place. God first called Abraham in Mesopotamia, then again in Haran. In Egypt he remained with Joseph, rescued him and elevated him to become a ruler. God saved Moses from death in Egypt and called him to special service when he was in the Sinai peninsula. That spot, far away from Jerusalem, was declared to be holy ground! The Lord also rescued His people with won-

ders and miraculous signs in Egypt, at the Red Sea and
in the desert! Clearly God was not limited to Palestine.

A second theme was that God called His servants to
move out from the place of security and comfort in
response to His voice. To Abraham he said, "Leave
your country, your people and your father's household
and go to the land I will show you" (Gen. 12:1). To
Moses he said, "I am sending you to Pharaoh" (Exod.
3:10). To be God's people involved moving out in obedience instead of seeking privilege and avoiding change.
This was necessary because God Himself was always
on the move, doing a new thing. This God called His
worshipers to be a pilgrim people.

Although Stephen did not attack the Temple
directly, it seems clear that he considered the Tabernacle, not the Temple, a proper symbol for Israel. God
directed Moses to build the Tabernacle according to a
specific pattern. The people carried it with them during
their formative period in the desert after God had rescued them in the Exodus. Under Joshua it was brought
with them into the new land as their enemies were
driven out. The Tabernacle, not the Temple, symbolized what the true Israel was to be, a people on the
march, responsive to God's call.

For the Lord was the God of the new, always going
beyond what His people expected and hoped for. He
was always doing the unexpected, working in the most
unusual circumstances. He could not be pinned down or
boxed in by ritual, Temple or Law. Now the greatest of
the mighty acts promised by God in the past had taken
place. He had sent the Promised One, a prophet like
Moses but far greater (see Acts 7:37; Deut. 18:15).

Along with the primary themes of God's gracious
acts and the obedience of Abraham, Joseph and Moses,
a dark thread was woven into Stephen's narrative. This
motif showed Israel's constant rejection of leaders

which God had given them and, ultimately, of God Himself. Out of jealousy the patriarchs had rejected Joseph and sold him into slavery. It was only by His sovereign grace that God used that sin to rescue the Israelites from starvation later on. Again God miraculously preserved His special leader, Moses, but the people rejected him at first, forcing him to flee to Midian. Even after he led them out of slavery the fathers rejected him, turning back to Egypt in their hearts. Still worse, their rejection of Moses meant rejection of God and they began to worship an idol made by their own hands.

Consistently appealing to their own Scriptures, Stephen quoted Amos 5:25-27, showing their idolatry in the desert was not temporary; it continued. Was he implying that they continued their idolatry by worshiping the Temple in place of God? As Isaiah said, "The maker of all things could not be limited to anything made by man" (see Isa. 66:1,2).

The climax focused on the theme of rejection. Stephen's hearers were just like their fathers who, resisting the Holy Spirit, had persecuted and killed the prophets. Now this generation had murdered the Messiah. As for the accusation of speaking against the Law, Stephen did not attack it; he only criticized Israel's failure to keep it. His words here remind us of Jesus' criticism of the Pharisees in Luke 11:45-52 and His parable of the vineyard in Luke 20:9-18.

Stephen was cut off before he could finish his address. But several implications were becoming clear. Israel would have to repent and believe in the Messiah or lose her position as God's special people. God was not limited. He was active wherever He chose and could be worshiped in places other than the Temple. Because obedience, not the mere possession of the Law and the Temple, was essential, God could have His people in other lands.

Thus Stephen had begun to lay the foundation for a much broader, universal understanding of the gospel. His ideas would soon find fertile ground in a most unlikely place, in the mind of a young Pharisee involved in his death.

Stephen's Tragedy and Triumph

Stephen, who had been remarkable for his spirit, his courage and his understanding during his brief ministry, became still more impressive at the point of death. He was given a vision of the glory of God, the glory that had dwelt in the Tabernacle and was supposed by his adversaries to dwell in the Temple. He saw Jesus standing at the right hand of God, apparently to confirm Stephen's witness on earth. His exclamation, "Look,. . . I see heaven open and the Son of Man standing at the right hand of God" (Acts 7:56) is especially significant. This was the last time the term "Son of Man" was used in the New Testament and the only time it was used there by anyone other than Jesus Himself. When the high priest had asked our Lord to tell under oath if He was indeed the Messiah, Jesus had replied, "I am. . . . And you will see the Son of Man sitting at the right hand of the Mighty One and coming on the clouds of heaven" (Mark 14:62).

The words were a reference to Daniel 7:13,14, in which the prophet saw the Son of Man being given authority, glory and sovereign power over all peoples and nations while men of every language worshiped Him. Thus at the hour of his death, Stephen's understanding of the gospel was confirmed. He was given a vision of the universal dominion of Christ and of the universality of His people. While most of the church, even the apostles, continued to participate in Temple worship and remained in Jerusalem, Stephen saw that the New Israel was to include people of all nations.

The crowd, unable to accept his message and possessed by blind rage, rushed at Stephen and seized him. What had begun as an orderly hearing became a lynching. They covered their ears to keep out the supposed blasphemy, dragged him out of the city, threw him down from a height and cast large boulders on him until he died. The witness (*marturion* in Greek) was faithful even to death.

His last words remind us of those of Jesus and show the degree to which Stephen was possessed by the Spirit of Christ. First he expressed confidence, "Lord Jesus, receive my spirit." Then he showed love, "Lord, do not hold this sin against them" (Acts 7:59,60).

Luke's description of the martyr's death amidst the stones is beautiful, "He fell asleep" (7:60). Stephen was a brilliant young theologian and a powerful orator. But it was not these gifts which made it possible to face his persecutors and eventually death with both courage and love. It was his confidence that Christ was risen, that Jesus was Lord, that His followers could trust Him completely in this life and beyond.

What a waste! How were the believers to deal with the double tragedy: the loss of a promising leader and the persecution which followed? For now the hostility which had been building against the followers of Jesus ignited into widespread harassment, imprisonment and scattering of the believers. And it was led by the most able and promising of the younger Jewish leaders, a Pharisee named Saul, who had been involved in Stephen's death.

The themes of Stephen's address help us here. God who is both powerful and gracious will not allow His purposes to be thwarted, not even by the disobedience of His own people. He is a specialist in turning sin into an opportunity for grace and apparent defeat into victory. Stephen had cited Old Testament examples of this gracious power, but the greatest in all history was the cross and resurrection. Now his own life and death would be another.

We recall that the young church, only a few years old, had settled down in Jerusalem. Apparently it coexisted with Judaism and was perceived by most as a heretical new "sect" on the periphery of the traditional religion. The apostles were no doubt faithful in their preaching and teaching of Christ but they seem to have forgotten, for the time, their Lord's mandate to go to all the world. And as Palestinian Jews they still could not understand that the New Israel must be freed from the Law and the Temple if she was to fulfill that mandate.

Stephen was doubly used to break the logjam. First came his understanding of the universal dimension of the gospel and its freedom from Jewish institutions. This would provide the first building blocks in constructing the theological launching pad for the wider mission. Secondly, his martyrdom and the subsequent persecution served as a goad, used by God to force the church out of Jerusalem so that it might carry its mission further. Thus the life, the thought and the death of Stephen became a gateway through which the Good News would be taken out to the world.

One of those forced out of Jerusalem into a ministry across cultural and geographical barriers was Stephen's colleague, Philip. The other man, introduced into the narrative here, was Saul of Tarsus, soon to become the most unlikely but the most effective apostle of all. We do not know all that was going on within Saul at that time. But we can be sure that both the message of Stephen and the manner of his death burned their way into his adversary's mind and heart. His pharisaical view of Scripture and history was challenged. He could not forget the confidence with which Stephen met death, especially the dying prayer, forgiving his assas-

sins. Saul could never forget that he had approved of
Stephen's death and even participated to some degree
(see Acts 22:20). Saul, a passionate seeker of truth,
devoted to the God of Israel much like Stephen was,
could not forget the martyr's witness.

Not only the thought but the missionary vision of
Stephen would take root in this most unlikely soil and
bring forth fruit. As Saint Augustine wrote, "The
Church owes Paul to the prayers of Stephen." Through
the most unlikely circumstances the Spirit had prepared
for the next steps in mission.

Questions for Discussion

1. Have you ever been a part of a Christian group
which considered itself religiously superior to others?
How did that make you feel? How do you think it made
outsiders feel? How should a group deal with this?

2. Write down all the ways in which the fullness of
the Spirit was shown in Stephen's life. Any surprises?
Does this expand your view of the ministry of the
Spirit?

3. How would you describe the difference between
Jewish faith and Christian faith, as you understand
them?

4. In what ways do you think Stephen and Saul of
Tarsus were alike? In what ways different? What do you
think was going on in Saul's mind as he heard Stephen
then watched him die?

5. What are the major themes you see in Stephen's
address? What new things do you learn about God in it?

6. Can you name other examples of God's power in
turning tragedy into triumph?

CHAPTER FIVE

Beyond the First Circle

Acts 8:4-40

Luke was a very careful historian. He did not recount incidents chosen at random, but inspired by the Holy Spirit, he selected each one carefully to illustrate how the same Spirit led the church into successive concentric circles of mission. Each time a significant new barrier was crossed it was the Spirit who clearly took the initiative.

Chapter 8 begins a transitional section in Acts that leads up to the launching of the mission of Paul and Barnabas in chapter 13. Before witness to the "ends of the earth" could be launched, Judea and Samaria had to be reached. This was true for reasons which were religious and cultural as well as geographical. Imagine how difficult it would have been at the beginning for believers to accept into the church non-Jews who did not keep the Law. It no doubt would have been impossible for the Palestinians especially.

We know that for the Jew all humanity was divided into two types of people—the Jews and the Gentiles, or non-Jews. But it was not really that simple. We have already noticed differences between Palestinian Jews and Hellenists. If we are to appreciate the outward movement of the church and the barriers it encountered and crossed, we need to understand other distinctions. Those who were not born Jews but had been converted, fully accepting and observing the Law, were called proselytes. Because they kept the Law and were few in number, the church had no difficulty in accepting them.

The Samaritans were a greater problem. They traced their ancestry back to Abraham in part and kept the Law of Moses. But they did not worship at the Temple (see John 4:20). For that and other reasons they were despised as inferior; however, they were not considered Gentiles.

Another group was called God-fearers. They were Gentiles who were attracted by the monotheism and high ethical standards of Judaism. They read the Scriptures and often worshiped in the synagogue but stopped short at circumcision and complete observance of the Law. Because the essential criterion of acceptance in Judaism was circumcision and the Law, not faith, the God-fearers were still considered outsiders. Jews could not have close association with them. This group would become very strategic in missionary strategy.

The final category consisted of all others, pagans who had no knowledge of the God of Israel or the Scriptures. A pious Jew could have no social relationship with a pagan. Knowing it is easier to leap over low hurdles than high ones, we can understand why the Spirit led the church to the Samaritans and God-fearers before going further.

The persecution after the death of Stephen was probably harder on the Hellenists associated with him than on the Palestinian believers. Perhaps this was why the apostles remained in Jerusalem; they certainly enjoyed the respect of the common people. At any rate, those who were scattered throughout Judea and Samaria "preached the word wherever they went" (Acts 8:4). The Greek word here is "evangelize." They proclaimed the Good News of Jesus. Luke passes over the witness in Judea in just a phrase. There was no religious or cultural barrier to be crossed here, only geographical and that was slight. The next hurdle was greater and would receive more attention.

Philip, who had been one of Stephen's co-workers, was no doubt influenced by his friend's understanding of the universal nature of the gospel. Like Stephen he was filled with the Spirit. A powerful preacher, he was used by God to do signs and wonders. Now he proclaimed Christ to the Samaritans with great success. This was one of the greatest manifestations of the Spirit the church had yet seen. He overcame ancient barriers of hostility in both Philip and his hearers.

We know from our reading of the Gospels that Jews and Samaritans had no dealings with each other. Their enmity was centuries old. Judah and Israel had separated after the death of Solomon. The Northern Kingdom, sometimes called Samaria after its capital city, had fallen to the Assyrians in 721 B.C. At that time their conqueror had deported many of the inhabitants, replacing them with pagans from elsewhere (see 2 Kings 17:24-41). This was common practice, designed to break any nationalistic spirit that might remain. The newcomers intermarried with the Israelites but were considered racially inferior by the people from Judah, now called Jews.

After the fall of Judah to Babylon in 597 and 586 B.C., many Jews were taken into exile. But they refused to lose their identity and became far more devoted to the Law and their traditions than before. Some returned to Palestine. The books of Ezra and Nehemiah tell the struggle of the returned exiles to rebuild Jerusalem and the Temple and to reestablish observance of the Law.

At the outset the Samaritans had asked that they be

allowed to help rebuild the Temple adding that they sacrificed to the same God. The Jews on the other hand
knew that intermarriage with pagans had led to the mix-
ture of idolatry with worship of the true God and
brought their downfall earlier. Considering the Samaritans to be both religiously and racially impure, they
rejected the overture. When the offer of cooperation
was rebuffed, hostility between the two groups esca-
lated. The Samaritans eventually built their own temple
on Mount Gerazim, but it was destroyed by the Jewish
king, John Hyrcanus, in 128 B.C. Thus the enmity
between Jews and Samaritans continued. (See John 4
and Luke 9:51-56.)

Philip was a Hellenistic Jewish believer, as we have
already seen. Thus he was an ideal person to reach out
to groups beyond orthodox Jewish circles. The Hellenists lived outside Palestine and were more accustomed to dealing with all kinds of people since they had
a more cosmopolitan outlook on life. Therefore the barriers between Philip and the Samaritans were no doubt
less than they would have been in the case of Palestinian believers.

Although they were unorthodox by Jewish standards the Samaritans also awaited the Messiah (see
John 4:25). Deuteronomy 18:15 was an important text
for them. Imagine the sensation Philip's message must
have caused in Samaria! Good news! Not only had the
Messiah come, he proclaimed, but now the Samaritans
were to be fully accepted into the New Israel. After
centuries of exclusion the barriers had fallen; they were
invited to become part of God's people on the same
basis as anyone else. They would no longer be despised
as second-class citizens!

The basis of their acceptance was also Good News.
Because of the life, death and resurrection of Jesus
there was no longer any need to quibble over fine points

of the Law or location of the Temple. Repentance and faith in the crucified and risen Messiah was the open door to salvation and life. The message was authenticated by clashes between the healing power of God and the destructive forces of evil. In these conflicts many were healed both of physical diseases and demon possession. Such "power encounters" would often accompany new breakthroughs in the book of Acts and all through Christian history.

With the message of the coming of the Messiah, their acceptance into the Kingdom of God and the evidence of God's power, it is no wonder there was great joy in the city. We do not know if Philip had formal authorization from the apostles or the Jerusalem church to baptize; we do not even know if that was considered necessary. But it was clearly the logical step, and Philip, led by the Spirit, baptized all who believed.

If the Samaritans had reason to be astonished, imagine the feelings of the Palestinian believers back in Jerusalem. Philip had just wiped out seven centuries of feelings of superiority toward the Samaritans! Could such a rash act be of God? Wasn't something more necessary before those unorthodox people could be accepted into the church? The importance of the question is shown by those who came to Samaria to investigate—no less than Peter and John, the top leaders of the church.

It is certainly to their credit that the two apostles did not attempt to hinder this new movement of the Spirit. Rather they affirmed it and cooperated with it. As Luke tells us, "Peter and John placed their hands on them, and they received the Holy Spirit" (Acts 8:17). No doubt the Spirit was manifested in some dramatic manner similar to that at Pentecost.

This incident puzzles many Christians and has been the subject of debate among scholars. Some see it as the beginning of the rite of confirmation used in some churches. They believe the Spirit comes only as the apostles or their successors, the bishops, lay hands on believers. But it was not always necessary for an apostle to be present for the Spirit to come (see Acts 9:10-19). Other Christians see these passages as proof that the baptism of the Holy Spirit is an event separate from and subsequent to conversion.

We can understand why the two experiences were separate for the apostles: the Spirit had not yet been poured out on the church until Pentecost. But Peter's sermon on that day seems to say that the gift of the Spirit comes immediately with repentance, faith and baptism (see Acts 2:38). However, two other incidents are recounted after Pentecost where baptism in water and in the Holy Spirit were separate. The first took place in the house of Cornelius and will be considered later. The second concerned the men in Ephesus who were disciples of John the Baptist and knew nothing of Christ. In all the other baptisms recorded, there is no mention of a separate baptism of the Spirit.

Now it is clear that the Holy Spirit was powerfully active in Samaria before Peter and John arrived. The power of Philip's preaching, the signs and mighty works performed through him and the conversion of multitudes all indicated this. None of it would have been possible without the activity of the Spirit both in Philip and in his hearers. But there was a unique need for a special manifestation of the Spirit on this occasion. We have already noted the intense, long-standing hostility between Jews and Samaritans. We have seen that all orthodox Jews considered Samaritans to be second-class, half-breed cousins at best. This feeling no doubt continued, in some degree at least, in the young church. As this crucial barrier was broken in the early missionary history of the church, God graciously gave a special sign. This is an important characteristic in Acts.

Each time a significant barrier was broken in taking the gospel out to the whole world, God gave some special manifestation of His power, presence or guidance. In this case the special sign of the baptism of the Spirit was necessary both for the Jerusalem church and the Samaritan believers. It told the Jewish believers that God had fully forgiven the Samaritans just as He had forgiven them and that the gateway to salvation was the same: repentance and faith in Christ.

The manifestation of the Spirit confirmed to the Samaritans the marvelous Good News of Philip's message. They were completely accepted into the New Israel. They were no longer second-class citizens in God's people; indeed there were *no* second-class citizens in the Kingdom of God! The reception of the Samaritan believers into the church was a powerful statement of the gospel itself and was the crucial step in expanding the horizon of the Christian community.

The Spirit and Simon the Sorcerer

The baptism of the Spirit brought a strange reaction in Simon the sorcerer. He had made his living by convincing the people that he had access to occult power. Seeing the genuine power in Philip he "believed," in some sense at least, and was baptized with the others. Whatever his motives it is clear that he wanted to be as close as possible to this new source of power. When he saw the manifestations of the Spirit which came through Peter and John he knew he wanted it at all cost and naively asked that he might buy the power from them. The apostles' indignant reaction was immediate and clear. Simon had missed the point of the gospel; his heart was not right with God; he needed to repent.

We may think it strange that Luke included this curious incident. But the story communicates a powerful message. First, the gifts of God, including the Holy Spirit, are precisely that—they are gifts. They can be purchased neither by money nor by good works. They can only be received as gifts from a gracious God to those who believe and trust Him. Secondly, there is a still more subtle lesson here. Simon wanted the gift of the Spirit and the power to confer it on others for all the wrong reasons, for manipulation not ministry. He wished to use the Spirit to manipulate those around him for his own benefit. This was the complete opposite of the reason for which God had poured out this gift. The Spirit had been given to continue the ministry of Jesus Christ in and through His people. The Spirit was not given so that some might control others; He was given in order that all believers might be free from self-seeking to witness and serve in the name of Christ.

It is worth noting that earlier, after the Jewish council had threatened the apostles and warned them not to speak, the apostles returned to the believers and prayed together. They did not ask specifically for the power of the Spirit; they asked for boldness in witness. The answer to their prayer was the filling of the Spirit to equip them for further ministry. In other words, the experience and power of the Spirit were not ends in themselves. They came to equip believers for ministry (see Acts 4:23-31).

Thirdly, we remember that the Spirit is Lord. He commands us; we do not command Him. He first brought Philip, then the apostles, to Samaria; they did not bring Him. They were His servants; He was not theirs.

The Spirit taught Peter and John an important lesson in Samaria. Before their experience with Philip they no doubt would have been most reluctant to preach to Samaritans. But now they shared the Good News in many Samaritan villages as they returned to Jerusalem.

Philip and the Ethiopian

Acts makes it clear that God guides His people in different ways. Neither His methods nor our experiences can ever be stereotyped. Philip had gone to Samaria to escape persecution and perhaps death. But God used him there to lead the church in a strategic step outward both in its understanding and implementation of world mission.

Having guided Philip by means of external events in the first case, the Spirit now did so through an angelic messenger who sent him to follow the main road south of Jerusalem. It led through Gaza on to Egypt and was a heavily-traveled trade route.

On the road Philip encountered the chariot of a high government official of Ethiopia. Different from the modern nation with that name, it lay along the upper Nile from Aswan to the south. Its people were black-skinned Nubians ruled by a queen mother who bore the title Candace. Since this official had gone to Jerusalem to worship, he must have been either a God-fearer or a proselyte. We cannot be sure which. It is most likely the Ethiopian was a proselyte, a convert to Judaism who observed the Law. Luke, later on, gives very special attention to another God-fearer, Cornelius, and his admission into the church (see Acts 10:1—11:18).

Cornelius represented the breaking of another barrier as the gospel continued to move out, but it was not yet that which separated Jew from non-Jew, those who kept the Law from those who did not. While there were men from Africa who heard the gospel in Jerusalem at Pentecost, this Ethiopian is the first specific individual from Africa mentioned in Acts. Thus his conversion represented one more circle in the expansion of the church. His race also pointed to the universality of God's purpose as He called together His new people.

The text (Acts 8:26-39) shows that the Ethiopian

was reading Isaiah in the Greek translation of the Old Testament, known as the Septuagint. Hebrew had dropped out of use except in the synagogues by the first century and was not even understood by most Jews, to say nothing of Gentiles. Thus the Greek translation, completed 150 years before Christ, was extremely valuable in preparing for the spread of the gospel. Because of it seekers of truth throughout the Roman Empire and beyond could read the Jewish Scriptures which pointed to Christ.

Again the Spirit guided Philip specifically. "Go to that chariot and stay near it" (8:29). People normally read aloud in ancient times; thus Philip heard the Ethiopian reading from Isaiah 53. The evangelist's sensitive approach, in which he was no doubt also led by the Spirit, resulted in an invitation from the Ethiopian for Philip to sit with him in the chariot. Philip, beginning with that passage, told the Ethiopian the Good News about Jesus.

The words in Isaiah tell of the Suffering Servant and constitute the most profound of all the prophecies of the Messiah. Undoubtedly Jesus had focused much of His post-resurrection teaching on this passage. He said, "This is what is written: The Christ will suffer and rise from the dead on the third day, and repentance and forgiveness of sins will be preached in his name to all nations, beginning in Jerusalem" (Luke 24:46,47). Now Philip, a participant in the process of the evangelization Jesus described, used Isaiah 53 as the springboard which took the gospel to the mind and heart of his host.

As they rode along and conversed, the Ethiopian understood and believed. Philip no doubt explained, as Peter had done at Pentecost, that repentance, faith and baptism were necessary to receive the forgiveness of sins and the gift of the Spirit. As someone has said, evangelism takes place when an honest seeker meets someone who is a willing sharer of the gospel. That well describes this event. Now arriving at a pool or stream, the Ethiopian showed no hesitation in asking for baptism. Verse 37 is not found in many New Testament manuscripts and was probably added early in the second century. But it does show the simple but clear confession of faith used in the early church.

Now the Spirit led Philip elsewhere. The African continued his journey south; Philip began to move up the coastal cities, preaching as he went, until he reached Caesarea. There he remained, giving leadership to the church and evangelizing the area round about (see Acts 21:8).

Philip and the Spirit

Philip was obviously a powerful evangelist, one who broke new ground in the missionary outreach of the church. He was also clearly guided by the Holy Spirit. Thus his life holds valuable lessons for us today. We find a healthy concern about the power and guidance of the Spirit in many modern Christians. They have rightly understood that Jesus is not an absentee landlord, that the gospel does not offer us just a compass or a road map for life. God's gift is a personal guide who lives within us.

Yet if this discovery leads us to focus on the gifts of the Spirit for their own sake, or for the ecstatic experiences which may accompany them, we risk falling into the selfish sin of Simon. The more we are filled with the Spirit, the more our focus will shift from ourselves to God. Equally, the more we are filled with the Spirit, the more our focus will shift from our personal concerns to God's purpose for His world.

There is a clear, consistent relationship between the work of God the Father in creation and redemption, God the Son in our salvation and God the Holy Spirit in bringing that redemption to lives today. Even as the Spirit brings the living Christ to us, blesses us with all His benefits and re-creates our lives, He does so in order to make us into instruments of His mission throughout the world. Both the internal and external aspects of the work of the Spirit are necessary. They cannot be in contradiction with each other. But the primary thrust of the Spirit is always outward to the world which desperately needs the love and power of Christ.

Philip is a helpful example for us. His driving passion was to be Christ's servant and witness. There is no evidence that he sought the activity of the Spirit for selfish reasons as Simon the sorcerer had done. Rather he sought to be faithful, first in serving tables, then in proclaiming the gospel. As he did so, the Spirit evidently worked in greater intimacy in his life and guided him very specifically at times. This guidance had to do not with Philip's personal concerns but with the mission to which Christ had called him. His example teaches us that the main prerequisite for guidance in any aspect of life is our commitment to be God's person and be involved in His purpose.

Expelled from Jerusalem by tragic persecution, Philip remained alert and open to the new opportunities before him. Refusing to give way to despair, he followed the initiative of the Spirit, leading the church to break through significant religious, geographical and racial barriers. New circles beyond Jerusalem and Judea were penetrated with the gospel. And more was to come.

Questions for Discussion

1. Have you seen the gospel overcome cultural differences and traditional animosities in your community? What could your church do to encourage it?

2. Describe all the ways in which you see the Holy

Spirit working in Samaria in this situation. Do you think any one act of the Spirit is more important than another?

3. Contrast the attitude of Philip and Simon toward the Spirit and His gifts. What application do you see for your own life?

4. What can we learn about effective evangelism from studying Philip's encounter with the Ethiopian?

5. What new aspects of the purpose and function of the Holy Spirit have you discovered so far in this study?

CHAPTER SIX

God's First Great Surprise: Saul

Acts 9:1-31; 22:1-21; 26:9-23; 11:25,26

It is clear that every time a new step is taken in redemptive history it is God who takes the initiative. The stories of Abraham, Moses and, above all, of Jesus Christ are among the best known examples. We shall discover others as we continue in Acts.

We have already seen how the foundation was being laid for mission to the world beyond Palestine and to peoples besides the Jews. Stephen, a Hellenistic Jewish believer, pointed the way to an understanding that the gospel was for all. His martyrdom forced many believers out of Jerusalem and resulted in the spread of the faith. Philip took the bold step of welcoming the despised Samaritan "cousins" into the church. But it was still unthinkable for most—if not all—believers that Gentiles who did not keep the Law could be accepted.

During centuries of struggle for survival, the Jews guarded the Law as the only bulwark against their loss of identity and disappearance as a people. Ingrained into every Jew was the equation: to be a part of the people of God was to keep the Law, to reject the Law was to reject God.

Now two mighty surprising acts of God were to prepare the church to accept all who believed in the Messiah, whether or not they kept the Law and were a part of Jewish culture. One was the conversion of Saul, the chief enemy of the church. The other was the conversion of Cornelius, an uncircumcised Roman. The first event will occupy our attention here.

Saul of Tarsus

The primary leader in the persecution of the church after the death of Stephen was Saul of Tarsus. His father, a strict Pharisee, had taken or sent him to Jerusalem to study under the great Rabbi Gamaliel, also a Pharisee. Devoted to the truth as he understood it, Saul sought to know and serve God with his whole being. He had accepted without question the traditions of his fathers.

We do not know if he saw or heard Jesus in Jerusalem. But it is probable that he heard Stephen speak in the synagogue and quite possible that he argued with him. We know he heard the martyr's final address and witnessed his death. Stephen's impact on Saul, even though delayed, can scarcely by overestimated. Saul's brilliant mind, well trained in the Scriptures, must have raced along with Stephen's, recognizing the accuracy and logic of what he said, even while rejecting his conclusions about the Messiah. The manner of Stephen's death, in which he gave glory to the God of their fathers and asked forgiveness for his murderers, burned its way into Saul's consciousness. The man's words might sound like blasphemy, but how could one deal with his confident attitude at death?

Though the witness of Stephen remained in his mind, Saul's zeal for the Law and his desire to preserve the nation against the undermining effect of the new faith led him to action. Enraged, he took considerable initiative in bringing about the imprisonment and death of believers in Jerusalem. To him they were blasphemers, teaching that a crucified and thus accursed man (see Deut. 21:22,23) was the Messiah. No measure against the believers was too severe. Not content to drive them out of Jerusalem he sought and received authorization from the high priest to persecute them in Damascus and other foreign cities where they had fled (see Acts 9:1,2; 26:11). This was legal since the high priest, with the backing of Rome, was considered head of the Jewish state for internal affairs. His authority also extended to Jews outside Palestine.

The journey took about a week on foot. We cannot reconstruct everything that went on in Saul's mind. But we can imagine that he could not shake off either Stephen's teaching or the manner in which he had met death. Saul must have had to recognize the validity of his analysis of the history of the Jews down to the present. The one totally unacceptable point was the conclusion, that the crucified one was the Messiah. Now the crucified and risen Messiah answered that objection by appearing to Saul.

A light brighter than the midday desert sun blinded Saul, and as he lay on the ground he heard a voice: "Saul, Saul, why do you persecute me?" Since Saul was persecuting the church and not some heavenly figure we can imagine his bewilderment. To his question, "Who are you Lord?" came the reply, "I am Jesus, whom you are persecuting" (Acts 9:4,5).

With these words Saul knew that Jesus was indeed the Messiah, that He had risen from the dead and that He identified Himself with His people. *Koinonia* was not just the oneness of believers with each other; it was the oneness of their Lord with them in their trials. No doubt Saul had a long way to go in his theological understanding, but now the witness of Stephen and other believers was confirmed. Jesus was Messiah and Lord!

In his account to Agrippa, Paul said that Jesus added, "It is hard for you to kick against the goads" (26:14). A goad is a long pole, sharpened at one end, used to keep cattle moving. Thus the metaphor suggests a rebellious Saul, reluctant to move forward in accordance with God's will, injuring himself as a result. Conflict raged within Saul.

What were the "goads" God was using in his life? No doubt one was the testimony of Stephen, already discussed. This included not only the manner in which Stephen accepted death, but his argument from Old Testament history. Another must have been Saul's conflict with the demands of the Law. A sensitive and profound person, Saul must have suspected by now that he could never fully live up to the Law. Perhaps, looking back at God's dealings with Old Testament saints, he began to doubt if that was God's chief concern. But up to this point the proud young Pharisee was resisting. He could not admit that he, as much as anyone else, needed grace, forgiveness and power. (See Romans 7:7-12.)

Although we do not know all that happened on the Damascus road we can be sure it was not a product of Saul's imagination. Those around him saw the light and heard the sound but could not comprehend what was taking place. While there were external aspects of the experience that others could see and hear, its real significance took place in the personal encounter between Saul and the risen Christ. We recall that one essential requirement of an apostle was that he be a witness of the resurrection (see Acts 1:22). Saul would always insist from this day on that he too was an eyewitness of the resurrection. The risen Christ had appeared to him personally and commissioned him to be His apostle (see 1 Cor. 15:8-10; Gal. 1:1,11,12).

It is clear that Saul's conversion was also a call to witness and service. His contribution as the great missionary to the Gentiles, to Asia Minor and Europe, would be unique. We do not know how explicitly Saul understood this at the beginning. The Lord told Ananias that this man was a "chosen instrument" to carry His name to Gentiles and their kings, as well as to the people of Israel. Saul added in his account to Agrippa that the Lord told him at his conversion that he was to be sent to the Gentiles (see Acts 26:17,18). Such a revelation may have been more than Saul could bear at the time; some think he telescoped later revelations into the account he gave to the king. At any rate it is clear that Saul understood, whether now or later, that his call to know Christ was a call to share Him with the Gentile world.

Ananias and the Impossible Command

What does one do with an impossible command from God? That was the dilemma Ananias faced. Saul, blinded but in obedience to Christ, went to a house in Damascus to wait for the next step. What a whirlwind of thoughts must have raced around in his mind! Had the experience been real? Was Jesus truly the risen Messiah? How could he be sure? What would he do now? What *could* he do now?

As Saul waited in the dark, fasting and praying, he received a vision in which a man named Ananias came, laid hands on him and restored his sight. But what about Ananias? This otherwise obscure man from the city was a devout Jew who had become a disciple. Imagine his perplexity and reluctance when the Lord told him to go to Saul. The Pharisee from Tarsus was dreaded throughout the churches for his persecution of the Jerusalem believers. Ananias had already heard that Saul planned to continue his campaign in Damascus. Ananias must have doubted that it was really the Lord who was speaking to him. And it does no violence to the text to believe that the disciple made every attempt to avoid such an apparently foolhardy mission. It is a measure

both of God's power and of Ananias's openness that he
finally obeyed.

The kindness with which Ananias approached the
erstwhile persecutor was astonishing. "Brother Saul,"
he said as he laid his hands on him (Acts 9:17). The act
confirmed the vision God had given to Saul, quieted his
fears and demonstrated the reality of Christ's love. Saul
was immediately filled with the Holy Spirit and received
his sight again. Without delay he was baptized, probably
by Ananias, and began to eat and regain strength.

Ananias disappears from the scene here. We know
nothing about him beyond what Luke tells us in Acts 9
and 22. But he will always stand as a reminder that to
be an obedient disciple of Christ involves risk. Little if
any significant ministry ever takes place unless believers are willing to overcome their fears and take risks as
they are led by the Spirit. Ananias also reminds us that
every great servant of God has been helped and influenced at key points in his life by obscure people. Like
the Moravians who witnessed to the discouraged John
Wesley and like the Sunday School teacher who led the
shoe clerk D.L. Moody to Christ, Ananias is another of
God's little-known but strategic people. We remember
the words of St. Augustine, "The Church owes St. Paul
to the prayers of Stephen." We can add, the church
owes St. Paul to the courage and faithfulness of Ananias.

Saul in Arabia
To understand the next events in Saul's life we must
look not only at Luke's account in Acts, but at Saul's
(Paul's) words in Galatians 1, and 2 Corinthians 11. The
latter give an expanded account of the events which
Luke summarizes in Acts. Luke reports that "Saul
spent several days with the disciples in Damascus," and
at once "began to preach in the synagogues that Jesus

is the Son of God" (Acts 9:19,20). In Galatians Paul writes that after his conversion he went immediately into Arabia and later returned to Damascus. After three years he went to Jerusalem (see Gal. 1:17,18).

Thus it seems that after his experience with Ananias, Saul was received by the Damascus church and for a short time remained there. The Jewish population of the city was somewhere between 10 and 20 thousand and it contained a number of synagogues. It is not hard to imagine the consternation and anger of the Jews when Saul arrived. Instead of persecuting the new, growing "sect" he had joined them! Instead of using his knowledge of the Scriptures to refute the message of Jesus, he too proclaimed that Jesus had indeed risen and appeared to him!

But Saul needed an extended time for study and reflection. He knew Jesus was the risen Messiah. He had accepted salvation as a gift through repentance and faith. How did those facts fit together with his understanding of rabbinical theology, especially the function of the Law of Moses? And where did the Temple fit in?

Thus after a very short time in the city, Saul went to "Arabia." This was not the modern nation by that name, but the Nabatean Kingdom whose northwestern border was near Damascus. He must have stayed there for some months, reexamining the Scriptures, remembering the message of Stephen and other Christian preaching he had heard. Above all he remembered his encounter with the risen Lord. Christ was the key who would unlock the Scriptures for him. He had to rethink his theology in light of the fact that the Messiah had come, been crucified and had risen again.

Saul came to a new understanding of salvation. It was not the result of keeping the Law or any other good works; it came only as God's gift by His grace to all who had faith. If this was true, what was the function of the

Law? It could not save, but it could lead the sincere
person to discover his need of a Saviour. And if this was
true it was clear that salvation could not be limited to
those who kept the Law. It was God's gift to all who
believed, Jew or Gentile alike. Thus in the desert outside Damascus, under the guidance of the Spirit, Saul
came to understand God's redemptive mission to the
whole world more deeply than anyone ever had previously. There he laid the theological foundation for the
church's mission to every nation, tribe and tongue. This
worldwide mission, seen as potential at Pentecost, was
now moving toward realization.

In his time of study and reflection, Saul must have
spent long hours in prayers and adoration. He could not
know all the dimensions of the task to which God had
called him. But Saul, nurtured in the Old Testament,
knew the path of God's servant was always difficult.
The great men of old, Amos, Isaiah, Jeremiah and others experienced rejection, suffering and even death as
they spoke the Word of the Lord to His people. Saul's
fate could be no different. Thus the time in Arabia, a
parallel to our Lord's time in the desert, was a period of
strengthening for the ministry to come.

Back in Damascus

After some time Saul returned to Damascus. His
primary ministry in the synagogues must have begun
now. He had originally set out with letters from the high
priest to these same synagogues. His goal at that time
was to discover any followers of Jesus among them and
send them to prison. Now he preached that Jesus was
the Messiah, the Son of God. No doubt he argued with
great power from the Scriptures and from personal
experience to prove the truth of his message. The
Jews, already furious over Saul's open adherence to the
despised sect, were now doubly enraged at his preach-

ing. Ironically, it was almost a repetition of Stephen's ministry in the Jerusalem synagogue. Saul's biblical knowledge and logic were so powerful that his opponents could not withstand him. This ministry lasted about three years.

Then the parallel to Stephen's experience was nearly carried to a tragic conclusion. The Jews determined to kill Saul and, perhaps to keep them content and maintain order, the governor agreed to help (see 2 Cor. 11:32). The city walls were guarded to prevent Saul's safe exit. However, one of those converted through his ministry apparently had a house on the city wall. The Jews and government officials were searching the city and guarding the gates but the believers saved Saul's life and future ministry. They lowered him to the ground, outside the wall, in a basket through a window at night and he went to Jerusalem. In his first three years of ministry, Saul learned that discipleship was costly and dangerous.

Saul and Barnabas in Jerusalem

It is not hard to imagine the suspicion and fear the Jerusalem church felt toward Saul. Spies who infiltrated a group in order to betray it were not unknown in ancient times. The believers in Jerusalem, still remembering with great pain the losses they had suffered because of Saul, simply could not believe he was sincere in his profession of faith in Christ. They gave no credence to stories of his conversion and ministry in Damascus; that all took place far away. But the believers felt firsthand the results of Saul's hatred and destruction in Jerusalem! Saul's dilemma was made worse by the fact that his former associates in the Sanhedrin and among the Pharisees regarded him as deluded or a traitor. Rejected by the church, the object of hatred from the Jews, he had no place to turn.

At this point Barnabas appeared on the scene again, showing why he was called "son of encouragement" or the "alongside person." He stood with Saul, believed him and encouraged him. Barnabas was held in such respect by the apostles that finally Saul was accepted in the church.

We have no way of knowing if Barnabas had been acquainted with Saul earlier. Perhaps he had been and knew him to be such an honest person that deceit was inconceivable. More likely Barnabas had deep confidence in the gospel and its power and knew that no one was outside its reach. This led him to risk his reputation in the church and perhaps his life by standing with Saul. Later Barnabas would launch Saul into his most important ministry (see Acts 11:25). Still later he would break with the apostle in order to stand with another man whom Saul himself had rejected. That was Mark whose courage failed at a crucial point on their first missionary journey, leading him to desert his companions (see Acts 15:36-39). Yet Barnabas again acted as the alongside person, the son of encouragement. To Barnabas we owe in large measure the ministries of both men.

Saul's ministry in Jerusalem at this time was brief. He showed his courage by debating in the Greek-speaking synagogues. Among them no doubt was the one where Stephen spoke and from which he was taken to his trial and death. The worshipers in the synagogues must have been furious. Stephen had been bad enough. Saul was worse! He betrayed those who had followed him as their leader in suppressing the new sect. Again the apostle almost met Stephen's fate. Again the Lord intervened: He appeared to Saul as he prayed in the Temple and told him to leave Jerusalem. There was abundant Christian witness in that city for all who were seeking the truth. God had much more important and far-reaching work for Saul elsewhere. With the help of other believers Saul went to Caesarea and from there took a ship to Tarsus.

The church in Palestine, its chief persecutor now a convert, enjoyed a period of peace and growth. It had spread during the persecution to Galilee as well as Judea and Samaria.

Saul in Tarsus

After he went to Tarsus Saul seems to have dropped out of sight for nine or ten years. We hear no more of him until Barnabas found him and took him to Antioch. Although we do not have as much information as we wish, we do have some evidence about his life.

It is probable that he was disinherited by his family in Tarsus. Acts 11:25 indicates that Barnabas had great difficulty in finding Saul, even though his family was prominent in the Jewish community and enjoyed Roman citizenship. In Philippians 3:8 Paul wrote that he had "lost all things" for Christ's sake.

We cannot believe Saul was silent or inactive during those years. He no doubt continued his ministry among Jews in Tarsus and the surrounding area. We do not know if he had already begun to preach to the Gentiles. But later on, when Barnabas faced the challenge of leading the Antioch church which included both Jew and Gentile converts, he thought of Saul. Does this mean that Barnabas knew Saul had already begun to reach out beyond the synagogue and evangelize non-Jews? It is quite possible that Saul already understood his call from the risen Christ in that sense.

Some of the churches in Syria and Cilicia, the province in which Tarsus was located, must have been established during that period (see Acts 15:41). It is probable that during this period he endured some of the sufferings he describes in 2 Corinthians 11.

Certainly Saul's study of the Old Testament Scriptures continued. Now Christ was the key who unlocked them. The seeds planted first by Stephen, then nurtured by the risen Christ, were growing into the understanding of the gospel that would shape both the thought and the mission of the church in the centuries to come.

Meanwhile Saul may have believed he had found his primary place of witness and service. But God had a far greater plan and during these hidden years the Holy Spirit was preparing Saul for a crucial role in it.

Questions for Discussion

1. Try to reconstruct the thoughts in Saul's mind as he journeyed to Damascus. To what extent do you think God used the witness of Stephen's message and death in his life?

2. Read the three accounts of Saul's conversion. What are its major points? What factors do you think are unique in this event? Are there factors which should be normative for every conversion?

3. Put yourself in the place of Ananias. What would your reaction have been if you had been there? What do you think led him to obey?

4. What do you think would have happened to Saul if Ananias had not obeyed?

5. Do you see a correlation between risk and discipleship? Do you think one can be a disciple without taking risks? In what way are you being led to take risks for Christ in your own life now?

6. Do you think Saul wondered if God had forgotten him during the years in Tarsus, failing to realize he was being prepared for something special? Have you ever felt that way? How can we deal with such feelings?

CHAPTER SEVEN

The Second Great Surprise: Cornelius

Acts 10:1—11:21

The conversion of Cornelius and his acceptance into the church was as unbelievable and shocking as that of Saul. In one case, the most fanatical enemy became a disciple; in the other, a man with whom Jewish believers and nonbelievers alike could not even associate was admitted into the family of faith. Here the greatest of all the barriers which separated the church from its mission to the world was shattered by a sovereign act of God. At the same time, He was preparing Saul/Paul, who would become His special instrument of that mission.

Luke must have had a wealth of material to relate in Acts. But his space was limited to that which a 35-foot roll of papyrus would hold. He no doubt agonized at times over what to include and what to leave out. So it is all the more impressive that the three events to which he gives the most space are the message and death of Stephen, the conversion of Saul (told three times) and Peter's encounter with Cornelius.

The three events were connected in the plan of God. We have already seen the impression Stephen made upon Saul, then his conversion and preparation for mission. Now God would lead, indeed almost force, the most respected of the apostles to accept an uncircumcised Gentile as his brother in Christ. All three events moved in the same direction. The falling of this barrier between Jew and Gentile implied the eventual destruction of every other wall of division—racial, linguistic, cultural and national—in order that the gospel might be taken to the ends of the earth.

The story may be seen as a drama with three main protagonists: Cornelius, Peter and God. It is God who takes the initiative throughout and brings the other two together.

Cornelius

Caesarea, located on the coast about 60 miles northwest of Jerusalem, was the seat of the Roman governor of Judea. Naturally a strong military force was kept there. Cornelius was a centurion and normally commanded 100 men. Known for their leadership, expected to be courageous and loyal, centurions were the backbone of the Roman army.

Cornelius was clearly an extraordinary man who sought God with all his heart. He contributed generously to those in need, he was a man of prayer, and his example influenced his family, his servants and even some of his soldiers. Most important of all, he was a God-fearer. Disillusioned by paganism and its immoral life-style, Cornelius was drawn to Jewish religion, probably attended the synagogue, lived by its high ethical standard and prayed to the God of Israel. However, he stopped short of the crucial dividing line between Jew and Gentile. He did not accept circumcision and the Law.

One afternoon as Cornelius prayed at the normal hour for devout Jews, God responded in a vision. An angelic messenger appeared, called him by name and told him to send to Joppa for Simon Peter. He immediately sent two servants and a "devout" soldier, apparently a God-fearer also, to the town 30 miles to the south. The fact that they arrived there the next day at noon shows they lost no time on the way.

Peter

God was working both sides of the street. This was such an important event for the self-understanding as well as the expansion of the church that God took special initiative with Peter as well as Cornelius. Indeed, the obstacle to be overcome in leading Peter to Cornelius was much greater than any in the mind of the Roman. A God-fearer had no scruples in associating with Jews, but no orthodox Jew would enter the house of anyone who did not keep the Law.

Peter had already taken a step or two away from strict observance of the Law: He had accepted the Samaritans. Now his host in Joppa was Simon, a Jewish believer who was a tanner. Since tanners worked with bodies of animals they were permanently unclean according to the Law (see Num. 19:11-13). Thus Peter's understanding of the gospel was growing. He could accept these "inferior" and "unclean" Jews as brothers in Christ. But both still observed the Law, living within the parameters of Jewish culture. The ultimate barrier between Jew and Gentile had not been broken. Now Peter's understanding of God's plan was to be expanded dramatically.

At noon, shortly before the three men from Cornelius arrived, Peter went to pray on the flat roof of the house. And God used his hunger to get to his mind and heart. The apostle was given a vision of a large sheet let down from heaven containing all kinds of creatures—four-footed animals, reptiles and birds mixed together. With the vision came the puzzling word from the Lord, "Get up, Peter. Kill and eat." "Surely not, Lord!" Peter replied. "I have never eaten anything impure or unclean" (Acts 10:13,14). Peter was shocked! The word from the Lord violated a lifetime of conditioning and centuries of tradition.

To understand Peter's reaction we need to remember that basic to the faith of the Jews was the belief that they were a separate or holy people. Circumcision and the Law both symbolized and maintained their separateness, a part of which was abstention from certain kinds of food. Some animals were unclean and could not be eaten (see Lev. 11:1-47). Even touching unclean food profaned a Jew. Consequently he could not enter the house of a Gentile where he would run such a risk. Nor would he allow a Gentile to enter his house. Thus, according to Jewish custom, Peter could never kill and eat the animals in the vision, much less could he enter the house of a Gentile and eat with him. As Peter puzzled over the vision and pondered its meaning, it was twice repeated.

Years earlier Jesus told His disciples that evil thoughts, not certain foods, made one unclean (see Mark 7:14-23). But the meaning of those words had been filtered out of Peter's consciousness by the preconceptions of Jewish tradition. Now through the servants of Cornelius who were just arriving, God would take Peter one step further in his understanding.

The vision was gone, but just as the Holy Spirit had spoken to Philip at another barrier-breaking point, now the Spirit spoke directly to Peter. He told him to go with the three men who had just arrived downstairs. The three Gentiles showed their sensitivity to Jewish custom by remaining at the gate.

When Peter heard of their mission he must have been astounded as he pondered his own vision and its connection to the message from Cornelius. What thoughts swirled around in his head? Perhaps the ideas of Stephen, perhaps even of Saul who wondered if God's people could be limited to the Jews. Certainly many sayings of Jesus came to the surface now which Peter did not yet understand. Could it be that Peter now remembered how Jesus had commended the faith of another Roman centurion (see Luke 7:1-10)? Did he recall Jesus' words in the Nazareth synagogue, reminding the people that God had once sent the prophet Elijah not to an Israelite but to a foreigner, a widow in Sidon (see Luke 4:26)?

Now, illumined by the Spirit, Peter suddenly perceived the meaning of the vision. His understanding made a quantum leap forward. He had seen many surprises since beginning to follow Christ: the crucifixion, the resurrection, Pentecost. Here was another on the same scale. God had broken the barriers between His ancient people and the Gentiles. All were welcome in the church! Peter's next step indicated the leap in his understanding. He broke with Jewish tradition, invited the Romans into the house, and offered them hospitality. We wonder what Peter's host thought!

Peter and Cornelius. Peter knew God was about to do something new, almost incredible. Suspecting what was about to happen he no doubt wondered how the Jerusalem church would accept it. So he took along six believers from Joppa to be witnesses and perhaps to give moral support as well. Cornelius, waiting in anticipation, brought together a group of relatives and friends in his house. No doubt he had told them of his vision.

The two groups met as Peter entered the house to face the expectant Gentiles. Two days earlier such a situation would have been inconceivable to him. But God had taught him an important lesson which he immediately shared with his hosts. He could no longer call anyone impure or unclean. Now he asked why Cornelius had sent for him. The Roman officer told of his search to know God, described his vision, and added that they were eager to hear everything the Lord commanded Peter to tell them. An amazing opportunity!

Peter began by sharing the revolutionary lesson the Lord had just taught him. God showed no favoritism but accepted those from every nation who feared Him and practiced righteousness. The Good News, first given to Israel, was that peace had come through Jesus Christ, Lord of all. While the term Christ was meaningful only to those who knew Jewish Scripture, Lord was a term that everyone there, God-fearer or totally pagan, would understand.

Now Peter proclaimed to these Gentiles the same Good News that he had preached to the Jews. The fact that the message was the same already indicated that the requirements for salvation and entrance into the church were identical for both groups. The clear implication was that observance of Jewish law and tradition could no longer be a condition of salvation.

Assuming that his hearers had some knowledge of the facts about Jesus, Peter outlined the events in order and told their significance.

1. God anointed Jesus with the Holy Spirit and power; thus Peter echoed Jesus' words in the Nazareth synagogue when He began His public ministry (see Luke 4:16-19).

2. As a result Jesus went about doing good and healing those under the power of the devil. No doubt Peter gave ample illustrations at this point, describing many incidents of physical and spiritual healing which he had seen.

3. The Jews killed Jesus by "hanging Him on a tree," the most disgraceful manner (see Deut. 21:23).

4 Then Peter emphasized the contrast between the act of men and that of God: Men rejected and killed Jesus; God raised Him from the dead!

5. This was not a myth; Peter and the other apos-

tles were chosen by God to be witnesses of this event. The resurrection was not the appearance of a ghost, a disembodied spirit. They had talked and eaten with Jesus after the event.

6. Now the risen Christ commanded them to proclaim this Good News to the people.

Peter began his message with a ringing, universal affirmation. Jesus is Lord of all! He concluded with two more. God had appointed Jesus judge over all as well. The Good News was that He who was Lord and Judge was also Saviour! As the prophets had predicted, God's purpose was that all who believed in Him would receive forgiveness of sins (see Isa. 53:11). This offer was for all; it could not be limited to Jews. The very nature of the message, that the one Lord over all offered forgiveness to all who believed, meant that the ancient barriers between Jews and non-Jews were shattered.

The Holy Spirit is given to Gentiles. Peter had already been surprised and his mind stretched by the events of these days. Now it happened again. Before he could even conclude his message the Holy Spirit came on all who heard it! This was accompanied with great excitement, manifestation of praise and speaking in tongues as they told of God's mighty works.

This is the second of the three incidents after Pentecost in which water baptism was separated from Spirit baptism. The first occurred with the Samaritan believers after the apostles arrived and laid hands on them (see Acts 8:14-17). This time it was quite different: The Spirit was poured out on the Gentile believers even as they were hearing and believing the message, before they were baptized in water or even openly professed their faith. It is clear that the Spirit is Lord; He blows where He wills (see John 3:8) and He cannot be limited or tied to any outward forms. No human plan was involved here. The Spirit of the risen Christ took

the initiative in opening Peter's mind to the new thing
He would do. The Spirit brought Jewish believers and
Gentiles together; the Spirit opened the hearts of Cornelius and his household. Now the Spirit, who continued to move in advance of His people, fell on the Gentile believers.

There was a special reason in this case. As Peter
felt himself drawn to this encounter with Cornelius, his
thoughts must have raced ahead of the events to wonder about their consequences. If these uncircumcised
Gentiles believed the Good News, what then? Logically
they would want to enter the church. If so, should he
require them to become Jewish proselytes, be circumcised and observe the Law, *before* they could become
followers of Christ? His Jewish background said yes.
Remember that Peter and the Jerusalem believers still
saw the church, the New Israel, as a group within Judaism. But the apostle's growing understanding of the
gospel said no, they should not be circumcised.

There was a second question: If Peter did understand the implications of the Good News that salvation
was by faith alone and did baptize this group of Gentiles, what would the staunch Law-keeping believers in
Jerusalem say? Surely the church would become
embroiled in bitter controversy and probably split.
Thus Peter's new understanding of the gospel and his
desire to maintain the peace and unity of the church
were in deep conflict.

We know this was not the end of the matter. This
would soon become the most critical issue the early
church faced. Even Peter later vacillated in the matter
(see Gal. 2:11-13).

But now the conflict in Peter's mind was resolved
by the surprising act of the Spirit. Poured out on the
uncircumcised Gentiles He clearly put His seal of
approval on their acceptance *as they were,* on the basis

of faith alone. Peter and the believers were astounded and convinced. Recognizing that God accepted the Gentiles completely, along with Jews, they could not deny baptism. The question of circumcision apparently was not raised. The Spirit had spoken, they must obey.

Peter and the accompanying believers baptized Cornelius, his extended family and friends. Then the apostle remained to teach Cornelius and friends for some days. Perhaps he wanted to put off facing the barrage of criticism that surely awaited him in Jerusalem. No doubt it was far more pleasant to teach these eager new believers in the house of Cornelius.

Peter's Defense in Jerusalem

Meanwhile, imagine the furor back in Jerusalem! The news of the reception of the Gentiles reached there before Peter did. The majority of the Jerusalem believers were Palestinian Jews who still thought it inconceivable that God would accept Gentiles who did not keep the Law.

Luke introduces a term here which we must understand. In the *New International Version* of the Bible, which we have been using, the opposition is simply called "the circumcised believers." However in the Greek the term is "those of the circumcision" (Acts 11:2). This indicates they were a particular party in the church. Imagine the temerity of this group which dared criticize the leader of the apostles! Many of them had been converted through Peter's sermon on Pentecost. He had baptized a number of them. They had seen his courage when he faced the Jewish council; they had seen the wonders God had done through him. Who was this group and why did they criticize Peter?

They were Jews who believed in Jesus as the Messiah but to whom it was still inconceivable that God could accept anyone who did not keep the Law. It is not too harsh to say they were Jews first and Christians second. They believed in Jesus but forced all His ministry and teaching to fit within the framework of their traditional culture. Anything that did not fit within that framework, the Lord's praise of the non-Jews' faith, His acceptance and forgiveness of those who did not keep the Law, was simply forgotten or ignored. Jesus for them was strictly a Jewish Messiah—if anyone else wanted to follow Christ he must first become a Jew.

Along with this theological concern the more conservative believers in Jerusalem feared for their relationship with the larger Jewish community. After the early initial period of favor with the people and hostility from the authorities, Stephen appeared. His understanding of the gospel and its implications brought persecution so that many believers were scattered. Some of those who remained in Jerusalem learned to live in peace with their neighbors by stressing their total adherence to the Law. Now the act of Peter in eating with Cornelius and baptizing him seemed to threaten the hard-won peace as well as the unity of the church.

Peter must have felt that he had been called on the carpet. He took the only approach possible. He simply recounted from beginning to end the whole incident—the importance of the event is indicated by Luke's repetition of the whole story. Peter also brought with him to Jerusalem the six believers from Joppa who had accompanied him to Caesarea. In Roman law, which the Jews knew, seven seals were necessary to authenticate an important document. Thus the apostle simply told what God had done in the presence of seven witnesses. He concluded with the account of the outpouring of the Holy Spirit. God gave the Spirit to these Gentiles, just as He had done to the Jewish believers at Pentecost! The church could not oppose what God had done!

The majority accepted Peter's defense and with

great awe praised God that He granted salvation even
to the Gentiles. Some however remained unconvinced.
Perhaps they were willing to see Cornelius as an
exception but not to accept the principle involved as a
general rule. At any rate, the problem would continue
to plague the church (see Acts 15:1; Gal. 2:11-14). It is
possible that the persecution which broke out soon
after, costing the life of James the brother of John,
arose because the church was perceived to be breaking
with Jewish tradition (see Acts 12:1-4). If so, the
acceptance of Gentiles must have been a major factor.

Progress in understanding and expansion of the
gospel never comes without struggle and conflict. This
breakthrough to the Gentiles was no exception. But it
set the stage for a most strategic chain of events.

Antioch: The Next Step to the Gentile World

Tucked away in Acts 11:19-21, almost as a footnote
to the encounter of Peter and Cornelius, is the story of
the beginning of the church in Antioch. A logical conse-
quence of the action of Peter, this event was another
important step in the process of world evangelization.
For Antioch would soon become the new base of mission.

Many believers, scattered after the death of
Stephen, shared the gospel in more distance places:
Cyprus in the eastern Mediterranean, Phoenicia up the
Palestinian coast and Antioch further north.

Antioch was the third largest metropolis in the
Roman world, surpassed only by Rome and Alexandria.
A beautiful city, it stood 15 miles from the mouth of the
Orontes River. It was famed for its pursuit of pleasure
through sports, gambling and temple prostitution.

Although most of the scattered disciples preached
only to Jews in Antioch and elsewhere, a few bold
believers, Hellenists from Cyprus and North Africa,

began to tell the Good News to pagan Greeks also. This was most significant. Philip had preached to the Samaritans but they were half Jewish. Peter had gone to Cornelius but Cornelius (and God) had taken the initiative. But now these unknown believers seized the initiative and went to Gentiles without waiting for an invitation. They must have found great spiritual hunger and receptivity. Many Gentiles believed and a mixed church, with both Jewish and Gentile believers, was formed. Its future importance could scarcely be overestimated.

This important breakthrough was made by persons whose names are unknown to us. A few years ago the Miami Dolphins football team was famed for its "no name defense," a group of players who were very effective but who were not well-known as individuals. Here the "no name offense" of the church was in action, people who were very effective in a strategic spot but who remain unknown to us. So it has always been. Alongside the well-known leaders God has always called and effectively used many more "ordinary" believers who never became known to history. We are called to be among them.

The Significance of the Cornelius-Peter Encounter

Some scholars speak of a "Samaritan Pentecost" and a "Gentile Pentecost" which followed the Jerusalem Pentecost. We cannot do so in any absolute sense, of course. The first Pentecost, when the Spirit was poured out on all believers, was unique. But there is a sense in which the terms are correct. The Spirit came on the Jerusalem church to prepare and empower it for its mission. Afterward, by coming on the Samaritan believers and then on the Gentiles so clearly and dramatically, the Spirit enlarged the church's understanding of its mission and prepared it for the next steps.

The Spirit of the risen Christ was continuing to lead His church beyond Jerusalem and its familiar Jewish culture to other peoples, places and cultures—to the ends of the earth.

Questions for Discussion

1. Do you see any people in our society who could be compared to God-fearers? How can you reach out to them?

2. Most Jewish believers assumed Gentiles could not become believers. Can you think of any groups in your community whom most Christians assume cannot come to Christ? What have you learned from the Cornelius story?

3. Imagine someone telling you he was eager to hear everything you had to tell him about God's Good News (see Acts 10:33). How would you respond?

4. Have you ever thought of the correlation between the universality of Christ's Lordship and the universality of His Body, the church? What does this imply for your own understanding of God's purpose in history and your own outlook on the world?

5. Do you see ways in which the Holy Spirit seems to be acting inconsistently in Acts? Do you see consistency in His action?

6. Are there prejudices you need to overcome in order to have fellowship with believers of other cultures?

CHAPTER EIGHT

Mission to the Gentile World

Acts 11:22-30; 12:25—13:52

One of the greatest indications of the presence of the Holy Spirit in anyone's life is his openness to the new movements of the same Spirit. Barnabas, whom we have already met, showed that quality often, but never with greater long-range consequences than now. The mother church, hearing of the conversion of Gentiles in Antioch, naturally wished to send a trustworthy person to evaluate the movement. Could these uncircumcised pagans be genuine followers of Jesus, the Jewish Messiah? In the case of the Samaritans, Peter and John had gone; at this critical moment, Barnabas was sent. The reaction of the Jerusalem believers would have far-reaching effects on history. It would determine whether the church would be confined to a small group within Judaism or whether it would become a worldwide movement.

The selection of Barnabas indicated that the church was learning to be more open to the new work of the Spirit. He was from Cyprus, just as some of the first evangelists in Antioch had been. He was a man of generous spirit and knew how to encourage new believers. He had even acted as a sponsor of Saul in Jerusalem.

We can imagine that he was overjoyed at what he found. As he worked with the local believers the church grew rapidly. Soon more leadership was necessary. The

church needed someone who was an effective evangelist as well as a good teacher. The Gentile believers,
unlike those of Jewish origin, had no knowledge of the
Old Testament. They were not used to living with high
ethical standards. Someone who was familiar with the
Scriptures but also knew Greek culture was needed to
teach them. The person should be at home both in the
synagogue and the marketplace, a skillful speaker to
communicate with Jew and Gentile alike.

Barnabas remembered Saul, the zealous Pharisee
who became an even more devoted believer. It had
been nine or ten years since Saul was sent back to Tarsus to save his life. Apparently there was little or no
contact with him in the intervening years. Perhaps
some scant reports, we do not know. Barnabas took a
ship to Tarsus to look for Saul. Apparently he was hard
to find. The Greek term translated "to look for," in Acts
11:25, indicates that. Perhaps he had been ostracized
by the Jewish community of which he would normally
be a part. Perhaps he was making evangelistic journeys
out from the city, establishing churches.

But Barnabas found Saul and brought him back to
Antioch where he soon became one of the leaders in the
church. For a year they worked together in ministry.
We can picture Saul and Barnabas evangelizing both
Jews and Gentiles in public places, then spending eve-
nings teaching small groups of new converts. They
must have been well instructed in the new faith.

Antioch was a cosmopolitan city, quite different
from Jerusalem. Here cultured Greeks, Jews, desert-
born Syrians and other groups mingled. Apparently
they all lived harmoniously together in the growing
church. As believers shared their faith, the term *chris-
tos*, or "anointed one" in Greek, became less a title as it
was for the Jews and was seen as a proper name. Soon
the believers were called, perhaps with derision,

Christ-iane, or "Christ people." Clearly the Antioch church was taking on its own unique identity.

Despite their different racial and religious background, the Antioch Christians knew they were one with all other believers. Thus when the prophet Agabus predicted a famine the Christians showed special concern for the mother church in Jerusalem. They made voluntary contributions and sent their gifts with Barnabas and Saul. We know the famine occurred in A.D. 46. We wonder if the Antioch church, by sending its two best leaders with the gift, wished to go the second mile to assure Jerusalem that its faith was genuine. After the two completed their task in Jerusalem they returned to Antioch, bringing with them young John Mark.

At this point the focus of Acts shifts. The center now moves from the more cautious, mono-cultural Jerusalem church to Antioch. There were several reasons. All or most of the believers now in Jerusalem were of Palestinian Jewish origin. James, who apparently replaced Peter in the local leadership after Herod's persecution (see Acts 12:1-19; 15:13-21), objected to the mixing of Jewish and Gentile believers. No doubt his desire to avoid offense to the larger Jewish community and minimize persecution led to special rigor in keeping the Law (see Acts 21:18-21).

But in Antioch it was different. The church lived in a very cosmopolitan environment. It showed great initiative in breaking down the barrier between Jew and Gentile. The Antioch believers were sensitive to the needs of others and sent relief to Jerusalem. Their leaders had lived in distant places and two of them, at least, already demonstrated concern for the mission beyond. Jerusalem would continue to be important but it was no longer the principal base of mission.

The primary figure from chapter 13 onward is no longer Peter, but Saul of Tarsus, better known as Paul.

Peter's ministry would continue to be important and effective but he would focus primarily on the Jews (see Gal. 2:7). Luke's (and the Spirit's) greatest concern is with the proclamation of the gospel to the world beyond, to the ends of the earth. And Saul/Paul would be the key figure in that process.

The Spirit Initiates the Mission

Each time a new barrier was to be crossed with the Good News, the Spirit of the risen Christ took the initiative in leading His chosen servants. The Spirit filled Stephen and showed him that the gospel would go beyond Jerusalem; the Spirit authenticated Philip's Samaritan ministry and led him to the Ethiopian; the Spirit brought Peter and Cornelius together. And now He would lead the Antioch believers to launch the greatest venture yet. Sixteen years after the resurrection He would use them to begin the movement that would not stop until it reached the ends of the earth!

The team of leaders in the Antioch church came from diverse areas and backgrounds. Simeon was a Jew but his other name, Niger, was Roman. Thus he must have moved in Roman circles and, as his name indicates, was apparently black. Many have wondered if he was the same Simon of Cyrene (in North Africa), who carried the cross of Jesus (see Mark 15:21). Lucius was from Cyrene and was no doubt one of those from Cyrene and Cyprus who first preached to Gentiles in Antioch (see Acts 11:20). Manaen may be the most fascinating of all. He was raised as a foster brother of Herod Antipas, the same king who ordered John the Baptist to be killed. What an amazing divergence in the paths these two boyhood companions followed!

This group apparently set aside special time for worship, fasting and prayer to seek God's will for themselves and the church. As they did so, the Holy Spirit gave them specific instructions. "Set apart for me Barnabas and Saul for the work to which I have called them" (Acts 13:2). The Spirit directed them to give their two most gifted leaders for the new venture. After further prayer and fasting the others laid their hands on those chosen to go and sent them off.

A New Creation: The Mission Structure

Barnabas and Saul were commissioned by the risen Lord and sent off after the church leaders laid their hands on them. This act did not add to their call or authority, but it was important because it symbolized the participation of the whole church in the mission. Through its leaders the Antioch congregation recognized Barnabas and Saul as its "sent ones." (*Apostle* and *missionary* both mean one sent out with a specific task.) In turn, the two missionaries continued to recognize their bond of *koinonia* with the whole church, but with Antioch especially (see Acts 14:26-28; 18:22,23). They were not under its control but they continued to be a part of the church. In turn they enjoyed its support in prayer and hospitality.

A new structure is introduced into the life of the church at this point, one with far-reaching effects. The local congregation, which we normally call a church, is located in one place and includes a relatively large number of people in all ages, married and unmarried, working in various occupations. Normally we use the word *church* to refer either to this local group, a national organization of congregations, or to the whole body of believers everywhere, the church universal. Most of us were converted and nurtured in such structures.

The new creation of the Spirit here may be termed a mission structure. Barnabas and Saul were as much a part of the whole church as before. But now they and their companions would not normally be part of a larger worshiping community, fixed in one place, including those of all ages. They would be a small, mobile, highly motivated group, focused on a particular aspect of Christian mission. In this case their call was to evangelize the Gentiles of Asia Minor and Europe. They would be used by the Holy Spirit to establish many local churches but would not become a permanent part of any of them. Their goal was to establish the church in a given place, leave it capable of functioning on its own, then move on.

Nearly two thousand years of church history make it clear that rarely has the Good News been carried across geographical, linguistic, racial or religious barriers without such mission structures. This is not to ignore the contribution made by those who have journeyed from their homes to distant places for various reasons, business, government, etc. and shared their faith as they went. But we know that most of the evangelization of Europe in the Middle Ages was carried out by various monastic groups which at their best were mission structures. In the sixteenth and seventeenth centuries Jesuits, Franciscans and Dominicans—missionary orders—took the Roman Catholic faith to large areas of the world. Beginning in the eighteenth and growing rapidly in the nineteenth and twentieth centuries, Protestants created special mission structures or "societies" to share the gospel. These planted congregations of worshiping, witnessing believers among those of many cultures and places.

Whether we speak of teams of Americans in Papua, New Guinea, Nigerian believers of one tribe and language going to another in the same country, or Mizo tribesmen in northern India crossing the Burmese border to evangelize Chin Hill people, the lesson is the same. The Holy Spirit will continue to call out highly motivated, mobile teams of men and women to share the gospel across barriers until in every tribe, race and culture there are those who call on the name of the Lord! Mission structures constitute a permanent part of God's strategy, and where the larger church has failed to recognize their necessity, it has been greatly impoverished and ineffective in its mission.

The Missionary Journeys

Again emphasizing the initiative of the Spirit, Luke indicates they lost no time in going to Seleucia, the nearby port, and taking a ship for Cyprus. It will be helpful at this point to summarize briefly the three missionary journeys of Paul, since there is not space to cover them in detail. The first, with Barnabas, is recorded in Acts 13:4 to 14:27. The second with Silas, began in Acts 15:40, ending in 18:22. The account of the third journey begins in 18:23 and continues until Paul's arrival in Jerusalem, Acts 21:17. His trip to Rome, beginning in Acts 27:1 did not start out as a missionary journey, but as we might expect became one, even though he was a prisoner!

Barnabas and Saul in Cyprus

Taking John Mark with them they soon arrived in Salamis, the island's main commercial center. Some of those who had first evangelized Antioch were also from the island. So it was logical that should be their first stop.

Luke tells us they proclaimed the Word in the synagogues for some weeks, but gives no details. However, we must ask why the great apostle, who understood that his call was to the Gentiles (see Gal. 1:16), invariably began his ministry in the synagogue, if one existed in the city he visited. Certainly there was an historical reason. Jesus was the Messiah of the Jews. They had the Old Testament which predicted His coming. They hoped for and expected the Messiah. Logically they should be the first to know He had come.

Paul's never-ending compassion for his own people was a second reason (see Rom. 9:1-4). But Paul was also a strategist. Could it be that he hoped that the majority of Hellenistic Jews, planted by God in the middle of Graeco-Roman culture, would accept the gospel and soon become witnesses to that Gentile world even as he and Barnabas were doing? It would have multiplied the church's witness very quickly. This obviously did not happen. But another group was present in the synagogue which would often prove to be receptive to the gospel. These were the God-fearers (see Acts 13:26; 17:4). In most cities the nucleus of the church would be formed of a few believing Jews plus a number of God-fearing Greeks. The latter then became an effective bridge into the greater Gentile community.

The three went on the island to Paphos where the Roman proconsul, Sergius Paulus, resided. It was a superstitious era and prominent men often employed their own private sorcerers. When the governor sent for the apostles and asked to hear their message, Elymas the sorcerer naturally feared his own influence would disappear. Paul, as he is now designated, filled with the Spirit and thus with the power of God, confronted Elymas directly when he opposed them. The result of this "power encounter" was that Elymas was blinded and the proconsul believed.

An important transition takes place in this first step of the mission. Saul is now called Paul. It was common for Jews to have two names, one Hebrew, the other Greek. The use of Paul's Greek name from this point on and its use in all of his letters no doubt are another indication of the major thrust of his mission—the Gentile world. At the same time Paul took leadership in the mission. From this point on he is mentioned before

Barnabas and becomes the principal spokesman. This is an indication of the greatness of both men, the brilliance and zeal of Paul, the self-effacing servant attitude of Barnabas.

The Mission in Galatia

Leaving Cyprus they sailed north to the mainland, landing at Pamphylia. Here Mark left the party. We do not know the reasons. Perhaps he was resentful that Paul had replaced Barnabas in leadership. He might have been frightened of the journey over the dangerous road to Antioch of Pisidia just ahead. It is possible that as a youth raised in Jerusalem he took a dim view of the focus on the Gentiles.

At any case, Paul considered Mark's departure a serious breach of faith and felt it disqualified the youth from further ministry. Barnabas and Paul would soon split over the matter but Barnabas, true to form, eventually led Mark into effective ministry. An ancient Christian writer tells us that later on Mark accompanied Peter and based his gospel on the preaching of the apostle. We also know that toward the end of his life Paul recognized Mark's value, asking that he come to help him in ministry (see 2 Tim. 4:11).

The missionaries left the coast, climbed the Taurus mountains and arrived at a plateau 3,600 feet above sea level. Here they entered the province of Galatia and soon arrived at a city called Pisidian Antioch.

The first Sabbath after their arrival the two entered the synagogue. As was quite common after Scripture and prayers, they were invited to speak.

This is the most complete report we have of any of Paul's sermons, so it merits special attention. It is helpful to put it alongside Peter's message on Pentecost and compare the two. Paul begins by reviewing God's dealings with Israel, just as Stephen had done. He focuses on Egypt and the Exodus, the giving of Canaan to the people and the history of the monarchy from Saul to David. Peter had also begun with the Old Testament background beginning with the prophecy of Joel because of its unique application to the giving of the Spirit. While the Old Testament introduction is different in the two sermons, each emphasizes the fulfillment of the ancient prophecies—the coming of Jesus.

The outline of the message is the same in each case.

1. The fulfillment of the Old Testament hope.

2. The coming of Jesus.

3. His condemnation by the rulers, who acted in ignorance. Both Peter and Paul see the cross as the fulfillment of Scripture, just as the coming of Jesus was.

4. God raised Him from the dead; He was seen by many witnesses. The resurrection was God's reversal of man's verdict. It was also the fulfillment of Scripture. Here Paul quotes Psalm 16, just as Peter did at Pentecost.

5. Forgiveness of sins is offered through Jesus to all who believe in Him.

There is a great similarity in the two sermons to this point. This shows us that the basic message of the early church was one. Peter and Paul, the two leading apostles, did not preach different messages. But as we would expect from men with varied backgrounds, there is a significant difference too. Peter had concluded with the Good News of forgiveness to all who repent and believe, as did Paul. However, Paul had been a Pharisee. The center of his religion had been to keep every detail of the Law and thus merit acceptance by God. His failure had added to the burden of sin. In turn he attempted to atone for sin by even more rigorous observance of the Law, only to fail again. Thus the Law had become an intolerable burden.

Christ freed a justified Paul from this vicious circle. Now the Good News was that Christ's forgiveness would free all others from this same burden (see Acts 13:39). This would become an essential element in Paul's message.

The sermon aroused great interest: many believed; others wanted to hear more. The message became the talk of the city. On the next Sabbath Greeks as well as Jews came to hear the apostle. Many Greeks present were probably not even God-fearers; they were pagans. Here we see the irony of the Jews' position. For centuries it had been their mission to glorify God in such a way that the Gentiles would believe. Now they were believing but their faith had come through these strangers who brought a message so amazing and liberating that Jews and Greeks alike could scarcely believe it. The majority of the Jews and their leaders could not accept salvation that was as open to Gentiles as it was to Jews—and put them all on the same footing.

Anger and envy instead of faith possessed them. They interrupted and contradicted Paul. He responded by quoting Isaiah 49:6 and announced he would turn from the synagogue to the Gentiles. This was a pattern to be repeated elsewhere (see Acts 18:6; 19:9). A number of Gentiles, including both God-fearers and pagans, along with some Jews formed the nucleus of the church in the city. From there the gospel spread throughout the surrounding area.

Not all the God-fearers believed. Some of them, women of the upper social strata, apparently resented the offer of free salvation to all just as the Jews did. They formed an alliance and used their influence to initiate persecution. Paul and Barnabas were expelled and went to Iconium, but they left behind them a group of new disciples filled with joy, despite the hardship.

Another circle had been penetrated with the gospel.

There would be many more. Like ripples moving out from the center as a pebble is tossed in the water, the Good News spread from each new city to the surrounding countryside.

We need to note another important factor. The church in Asia Minor was no longer culturally Jewish as it was in Palestine. Like Antioch, it included both Jewish and Gentile believers, all free to continue in their own traditional life-styles except for aspects which were contrary to the ethical norms of the Word of God.

But what did that mean? This was the crucial question the whole church would soon confront.

Questions for Discussion

1. If you were witnessing to people with no background in the Christian faith, as opposed to those with a Christian background, how would your message differ in the two situations?

2. After you shared the gospel with someone and led him to know Christ, what would you begin to teach him about the Christian life-style? What would your main points be?

3. What new characteristics have you discovered in Barnabas here? What does this teach you about the nature of Christian discipleship?

4. Name some mission structures you know. What kinds of barriers do they cross with the gospel? What unique ministries do they fulfill that are not carried out by local congregations?

5. How do you and your congregation participate in mission structures? Do you think this is necessary for well-rounded Christian discipleship?

CHAPTER NINE

Don't They Have to Be Like Us to Be Christians?

Acts 15:1-35

"What do you have to do to become a Christian? Follow certain rules, or what?" That was the question the writer once heard from a man whose marriage was falling apart and who knew that only Christ could help him. For the first time in his life he wanted to know Christ and follow Him. The early church had to face that issue and so do believers in every generation. There is always someone who prescribes a list of rules to be added to repentance and faith in Christ. The rules may be different but the problem is the same.

The Issues Involved

The great success of the Antioch church, and now the first organized mission to the Gentiles, raised this crucial issue for the early church. Some very conservative Jewish believers followed Paul to Antioch and Galatia. There they began to teach the new Christians that the only way they could be saved was to repent, believe in Christ *and* observe the Jewish Law. Circumcision was the minimal step in its observance. And as its most unique feature the word was really a shorthand term referring to the keeping of the whole Law.

Three closely related issues were involved, all dealing with the nature of the gospel, the church and its task. First, would the church ever be more than just a sect within Judaism? That would surely be the case if the Law had to be strictly observed. Some Gentiles would be accepted into an overwhelmingly Jewish church, but their number would be small. The church would see itself as a purified, faithful remnant of Judaism, the true Israel, which believed in Jesus as the Messiah. The place of the Gentiles would be limited, like that of the proselytes. If some more liberal thinkers allowed Gentiles to enter without totally observing the Law they would be second-class citizens in the New Israel, at best. There could be no universal church which sought men and women of every race and culture and called them to Christ.

The second issue was theological. It had to do with the very essence of the gospel. Must a person observe the Law, in addition to believing Christ, in order to be saved? If so, what was the determining factor, faith in Christ or keeping the Law? Clearly it had to be one or the other; it could not be both. If faith in Christ was the determining element, the Law could not be essential. If keeping the Law was necessary, the work of Christ was nullified and all people were back to the necessity of earning their salvation. In this case, the Good News was neither good nor news. We would be left with the old religious system from which Jesus came to liberate us.

The first issue is no longer with us. The second has cropped up repeatedly throughout history. There is a tendency in all of us to add "extras" to the gospel, to say we are saved by Christ *plus* something or other. But a third issue, much more subtle, has been still more persistent. It is the relationship of Christianity and culture. All of us are born and raised within a certain culture. This includes ways of dressing, eating, relating to others—in short, a specific life-style which we consider normal and correct. We see other life-styles as different and therefore inferior or wrong.

The gospel was first taken by Jewish believers, coming from their own traditional culture, to pagans whose culture was different in many respects. Most Jewish believers, without thinking much about the matter, assumed that of course pagans would be required to adopt their culture (which they believed to be superior) when they became followers of the Messiah. After all, that is what the proselytes had done.

It is difficult to disentangle the religious question from the cultural issue, but they are different. In one case we ask what is necessary for salvation? In the other how should a believer live and worship? For the strict Jewish believers the answer was the same in both cases. Life under the Law was necessary. But while the religious issue was settled long ago, the cultural question remains with us today.

Whenever believers from one culture take the gospel to men and women in another, the question arises. Should Christians in Nigeria dress, live and worship, build church buildings and sing hymns like the American Christians who evangelized them? Should new believers in West Kalimantan, Indonesia, adopt the style of life and worship of the Korean missionaries who brought them the gospel? Or should believers in every cultural setting be encouraged to work out styles of life and worship consistent both with the gospel *and* with their own cultures? Obviously this is a crucial question. We know it is God's will not only that the gospel be proclaimed to the ends of the earth, but that the church take root within every culture. God, who made all peoples, does not will that anyone should be forced to leave his own culture and become a part of another in order to follow Jesus Christ.

At the same time we recognize that every culture, while it has elements that are positive, also includes attitudes and practices that are clearly against God's will. This includes our own. Thus even as the Good News penetrates a given culture and is expressed within it, it will also begin to transform many aspects of that culture and life-style.

After this rather long introduction, we shall turn to events which led to the Jerusalem council.

The "Judaizers" in Antioch and Galatia

Imagine Paul's indignation and anger when he heard the news! Believers from Jerusalem, saying they had the authority of the mother church, had gone with a new command to those congregations where Jews and Gentiles were worshiping together, rejoicing in the breaking of the barriers between them. The command was that all Gentile believers must Judaize—become Jews in order to become Christians. Otherwise they could not enjoy *koinonia* with Jewish believers. They could not enter each other's homes; they could not eat with each other; they could not even celebrate the Lord's Supper together! But a still more serious issue was at stake. According to the "Judaizers," if the new believers were not circumcised they were not true followers of Christ; they were not saved!

This brought havoc to the churches. It threatened to destroy the fellowship and split the church into two mutually exclusive groups. It denied the heart of the Good News that salvation was a free gift received by faith. Even some of the leaders in Antioch were confused. Peter and Barnabas, sensitive to the scruples of those from Jerusalem, withdrew from table fellowship with Gentile believers (see Gal. 2:11-16). We can picture the bewilderment of the new believers in Galatia. It was the greatest crisis the church had yet faced, greater than the persecution under Saul of Tarsus. For while one involved opposition from outsiders, this revealed a fundamental misunderstanding within. This new threat, if not met and defeated, would so distort the gospel as to destroy it.

Paul dealt with the same issue in Galatians and many have wondered why that letter did not mention the Jerusalem council. The great New Testament scholar, F.F. Bruce, believes the letter was written from Antioch shortly before the Council took place.[1] This would explain why Galatians dealt in depth with the issue without mentioning the Jerusalem meeting, its decision, and its letter to the churches.

At any rate it was clear that the crisis had to be met by the whole church. It was not a local, peripheral issue. It was central to the understanding of the gospel and the nature of the church. Thus a group of Antioch Christians, led by Paul and Barnabas, went to Jerusalem to meet with church leaders and come to a consensus. On the way they visited congregations in Phoenicia and Samaria. There the believers who had been converted, mainly through Hellenists, rejoiced in hearing that Gentiles were being converted. This must have encouraged the Antioch group.

The Jerusalem Council

Paul and the others were welcomed by the church and repeated to the apostles and elders all that had happened. Since elders are mentioned with the apostles, a word of explanation is in order. The apostles were those chosen by Jesus of course. Because they were eyewitnesses of Jesus' ministry and resurrection, theirs was a unique, unrepeatable office. Their commission from the Lord was to the whole church and the whole world. It is clear that they did not exercise any authoritarian control over the church. The elders were no doubt the leaders of the local Jerusalem church, chosen by that congregation and ordained by the apostles.

James, the brother of Jesus, a strict observer of the Law, was their leader.

After Paul and Barnabas had told all that God had done through them among the Gentiles, a group of believers who had been Pharisees stood up and spoke. *Pharisee* means one who is separated. These men, prior to becoming believers, had separated themselves even from most Jews in order to keep every detail of the Law. Their code included not only the Law of Moses as originally given, but hundreds of minute interpretations which had grown up during the centuries. Although these former Pharisees now believed in Jesus as Messiah they continued to keep the Law themselves and taught that such observance was necessary for everyone, otherwise there was no salvation.

This group had understood only half the gospel. They believed the Good News that the Messiah had come. But they could not understand or accept the Good News of what He had come to do. They were not like Paul whose whole theology was reshaped by his encounter with the risen Christ. Their preconceptions blocked from their minds the offer of forgiveness and salvation to all, regardless of one's own merit. Since all or nearly all believers in Jerusalem were Jews who kept the Law, the views of the Christian Pharisees went unchallenged. If any Gentiles in the city had become believers, they no doubt had become Jewish proselytes in the process. These former Pharisees must have seen the incident of Peter and Cornelius as an exception, not the norm, justified because of the Roman's outstanding piety. They probably considered him and his household to be second-class believers. Perhaps they felt one exception could be tolerated. But now they recognized correctly that the mission of Paul and Barnabas would eventually change both the composition and the concept of the church.

After discussion Peter spoke to the group, which included the Antioch delegation, the elders, the other apostles, and a number of Jerusalem believers. First he recounted the story of his encounter with Cornelius, telling how God had taken the initiative in bringing them together. He must have told again of his vision in which God told him plainly that nothing He cleansed could be called unclean. He went on to remind them that God made no distinction between circumcised Jewish believers and uncircumcised Gentiles who had faith. God had seen the faith of Cornelius and his household even before they confessed it. He poured out the Holy Spirit on them and cleansed their hearts just as He had previously done to Jewish believers. How could the church demand more than God required?

As Peter continued he sounded a note of realism and probably echoed the feelings of most ordinary Jews against the Pharisees and their rigid interpretation of the Law. It was indeed a heavy burden or a yoke which was very difficult for an ordinary working person to observe (see Matt. 23:4). When a Gentile became a Jew and pledged to fulfill the Law, he was said "to take up the yoke of the Kingdom of Heaven." Perhaps Jesus had this in mind when He invited all who were overburdened to come and take His easy yoke upon them (see Matt. 11:28,29).

Peter's final point is theological. The Gentiles are saved by the grace of the Lord Jesus, just as the Jews. If free grace is the basis of salvation there can be nothing in addition.

Paul and Barnabas spoke next; Barnabas is mentioned first here because he was better known by the Jerusalem believers and still perceived as the leader in the missionary effort. Their emphasis was the same as Peter's although the events they recounted were different. When they had journeyed to Cyprus and Galatia

God performed wonders and signs among the Gentiles just as He had done among the Jews. The sick were healed, the lame walked, demons were cast out, believers were filled with the Holy Spirit. God showed His purpose when He poured out His grace, power and salvation on those who did not keep the Law just as on those who did.

Now it was time for James to speak. If anyone could be expected to take the position of the Pharisees it was he. He was the brother of Jesus the Lord and had not believed until after a special resurrection appearance (see 1 Cor. 15:7). A devout keeper of the Law, he was respected even by non-believing Jews. Thus his words would carry great weight.

James, perhaps for strategic reasons, did not mention the testimony of Paul and Barnabas but referred to that of Peter, calling him by his Aramaic name, Simon. Then he wisely went back to the same Old Testament which laid down the Law of Moses, quoting Scripture to show how from centuries past God purposed to call the Gentiles to know Him (see Amos 9:11,12). Then speaking not as the final authority, but rather giving the consensus of the group, James laid down the basic decision: they should not put any obstacles in the path of Gentiles who were turning to God. James may have been less enthusiastic, less aggressive than Paul and Barnabas on going out and seeking the Gentiles, but the primary point had been won. The essence of the gospel was kept and the integrity of the world-wide mission protected.

The Letter to Gentile Believers

But there was still the problem of the relationship the growing Gentile church had to the Jews throughout the empire—both those Jews who were believers and those who were not. This was a most delicate matter.

Paul was concerned to keep the stumbling block of the Law out of the path of Gentiles who were coming to Christ. In similar fashion, James wished to avoid offending Jews who would be repelled by the conduct of Gentile Christians whose life-styles appeared to show no respect for the God of Israel. What appeared to be freedom for one group looked like gross impiety to the other. The concerns of both were focused on the evangelism of Jew as well as Gentile. The removal of a stumbling block to one could easily create an obstacle to the other.

Secondly, the solution indicated a concern for the ethical standards of Gentile believers. The Jewish Law had to do not only with rituals and customs of a previous era, it also focused on the great issues of fidelity to God and justice to others. God's people were to reflect His character in their dealings with all. This was the point at which pagan society was weakest. Indeed it was such emphasis in Judaism that had drawn the God-fearers to the synagogues. Now that large numbers of Gentiles were responding to the gospel of grace and coming directly from paganism into the church, what would their attitudes be toward these ethical questions? How could they be led to follow a life-style consistent with the gospel without being given a list of rules and soon falling into legalism? Paul would later find he had to deal with this issue in his letters to Corinth and Rome.

When we see these issues we can understand that the solution in Jerusalem was not a mere compromise as some have said. It was an evenhanded decision that protected the integrity of the gospel, showed sensitivity to the Jews who loved the Law and began to lay down ethical norms for Gentile believers.

The Jerusalem council showed sensitivity not only in the decision but in its communication. The ministry of Paul and Barnabas was endorsed. Two respected lead-

ers from the Jerusalem church were sent with them to
confirm and explain the decision. They remained some
time in Antioch and their ministry there must have been
a strong demonstration of the unity of the church.

The letter made three recommendations. The first
was that they abstain from food sacrificed to idols. This
was a serious problem in the early church. Much of the
meat for sale came from animals which had first been
offered as sacrifices to idols. Only a small portion of the
meat was actually sacrificed; much of it was given to the
priests and then sold in the marketplace. Gentile Christians, used to eating this meat, might see little problem
in continuing to do so. But Jewish believers would consider the practice to be a compromise with idolatry.
Thus it should be avoided. Paul found he had to deal further with the matter in 1 Corinthians 8 and 9.

The second suggestion was that they avoid blood
and the meat of strangled animals which still contained
it. This was also a matter of great concern to the Jews;
to them the life was in the blood. The identification was
natural. When the blood ebbed away, life ended. Since
life belonged to God no Jew should eat anything with
blood in it. It was for this reason Jewish meat was killed
and treated in such a way that no blood remained.

The third requirement went beyond the ceremonial
aspect of the Law and possible offense to Jews to a
more basic issue. How would the gospel begin to
change pagan culture? What was the point at which to
begin?

Sexual immorality was a great curse in the ancient
world. Temple prostitution, both male and female, was
a regular part of a number of religions. It was common
in Antioch and Corinth especially. Sex for the male was
considered to be a bodily appetite to be satisfied at will.
No doubt many pagans believed in the gospel with all
sincerity and entered the church without understanding

the implications of the gospel for their sexual relationships. We have already seen that it was not God's will that men and women should leave their own culture and become Jews in order to become Christians. The gospel needed to take root within Graeco-Roman culture. But it would not leave that culture unchanged. It would begin a process, often slow and irregular, in which such practices as slavery, the exposure of unwanted infants and gladiatorial combats would eventually be abolished. The insistence on sexual morality was the first step because it was so all-pervasive and important in determining attitudes and relationships in the family and throughout society.

The church, led by its two strongest congregations, each representing different poles on the issue, had met its first great theological crisis. It was also a missiological crisis. For the theological answer given would determine not only the nature of the message but whether or not the church could continue its mission to the ends of the earth with any effectiveness.

In its decision, the church reaffirmed the gospel. It also was forced to a deeper understanding of the Good News, that its invitation was to everyone regardless of his culture. It opened the way to worldwide mission by affirming that men and women of every race and tribe can accept the gospel, worship and serve Christ without leaving the culture in which they were born. They are not required to adopt the culture of those who take the gospel to them, whether they are Jews, Americans or Koreans. The diversity and universality of the church was thus assured and the way left open to continue the witness to new people and places.

Questions for Discussion

1. Have you ever considered the expectations your church puts on new believers? Which of them come

from your own evangelical subculture, which from Scripture?

2. Are there some "extras," in addition to repentance and faith in Christ, that you or your church emphasize? What are they? Why are they there?

3. If you were designing a new church from the ground up for converts from contemporary secular American culture, what would it look like? List the essential characteristics in its life.

4. If you worshiped in a church of a culture very different from your own and found the service just like the one "back home," would you be pleased? Why or why not?

5. Name two or three issues on which you think the Holy Spirit wants to change American culture in light of the gospel. Are attitudes toward possessions, sex and people of other races among them?

Note
1. F.F. Bruce, *The Book of Acts* (Grand Rapids: Wm. B. Eerdmans Publishing Co., 1956), pp. 298-300.

CHAPTER TEN

Another Geographical Barrier Broken

Acts 15:35—16:40

The key decision was now made, the truth recognized. The gospel was a gift freely offered to those of every culture, the church would be a universal body, open to all. Where would the next circle of expansion lie?

After returning from Jerusalem with the good news of the decision, Paul and Barnabas remained in Antioch for some time. By now the leadership was stronger; many others were teaching and preaching and the church was growing. Paul wished to visit and encourage new churches in Galatia that were facing persecution and were confused by the controversy over circumcision. They needed to hear firsthand the decision from Jerusalem. Beyond Galatia surely the Spirit would lead to new areas.

Barnabas agreed with the proposal but wanted to take Mark again. Paul refused and the two disagreed so sharply that they parted and never worked together again. Barnabas and Mark went to Cyprus to continue their ministry while Paul took Silas with him to Cilicia and on to Galatia.

How are we to evaluate this distressing incident? Who was right? It is clear that even the greatest of the apostles were imperfect, stumbling at times as they attempted to be faithful. Paul in his zeal could not accept one who had deserted when things were hard. Perhaps he was too harsh and unforgiving, but he knew the younger man must be held accountable. Barnabas had the special gift of graciously accepting the underdog, standing by him and helping him to grow to maturity. His gift was put to good use here. But just as God had previously used persecution to multiply evangelism outside of Jerusalem, He used controversy to increase the missionary efforts. Now there were two teams where before there had been one, and reconciliation eventually came. Paul later recognized the great value of both men (see 1 Cor. 9:6; 2 Tim. 4:11).

Back to Galatia: Timothy

Paul and Silas first visited the churches in Syria and Cilicia, the region which included Tarsus as its major city. Since there is no record of the establishment of these churches some believe they were the result of Paul's work during those silent years in Tarsus, after he fled from Jerusalem (see Acts 9:29,30). Paul and Silas traveled from there to Galatia, going from church to church telling of the Jerusalem decision. As they went they also continued to instruct the church leaders and people in the faith while aiding their outreach to nonbelievers, both Jews and Greeks.

In Lystra Timothy, a new team member, was added. The young man would become like a son to Paul. Timothy's father, now deceased, had been a Greek; his mother and grandmother, probably converted on Paul's first visit there five years earlier (see 2 Tim. 1:5), were Jewish. The strict Jews refused to accept a mixed marriage and anyone involved was considered dead. Among the more liberal Hellenistic Jews who accepted such a union, the children took their identity through their mother. Thus Timothy would normally be considered a Jew. But he had not been circumcised. This created a dilemma for Paul. He wanted to take this promising youth along, to train him and to have his help in the work. But like a man without a country, Timothy was considered a Jew by the Greeks, while the Jews looked on him as a Gentile.

Paul resolved the question by having Timothy circumcised. Some have accused the apostle of inconsistency, especially since the Jerusalem council stated that circumcision was not necessary for salvation. But that was not the issue here. Paul's concern was not for Timothy's salvation; the act was irrelevant to that. His concern was for the most effective possible communication of the gospel to both Jew and Greek! Uncircumcised, Timothy would be an offense to Jews, seen as one who had rejected their culture. Now he would be recognized as one who identified himself with their traditions, who belonged to them. Having affirmed his identity as a Jew Timothy could more easily recognize his Greek heritage as well. Thus Paul turned a potential liability into an asset. Timothy would be a "bridge" person, a symbol of the breaking of cultural and religious barriers by the gospel to form one new man in Christ.

Paul battled to the end against any legalism which would compromise the nature of grace, the free gift of salvation in Christ. But once the battle was won he would go to any length possible in identifying himself with Jewish culture—or any other—to win people to Christ. "Though I am free and belong to no man, I make myself a slave to everyone, to win as many as possible. To the Jews I became like a Jew, to win the Jews" (1 Cor. 9:19,20). This was Paul's principle, to identify himself as closely as possible with those of any culture—as long as the gospel was not compromised—to win them to Christ.

The guidance of God does not always come easily, even to those most committed to His cause. At times it came clearly and specifically to Paul and his companions; at other times it came only after false starts and frustrations. Now Paul and his companions planned to enter the important Roman province of Asia, whose capital city was Ephesus. This must have seemed a logical step. For reasons we do not know they were prevented from doing so but recognized the guidance of the Holy Spirit in the matter. Next they attempted to go north into Bithynia, another important province. The Spirit again prevented them, whether through inner conviction, a vision or external circumstances we do not know. This left them with two alternatives, turn back or go further west. As we would expect they turned west and soon arrived in Troas, a city on the Aegean Sea, 10 miles south of ancient Troy.

Another Circle: Europe

Two significant events took place in Troas. First, Paul had a vision of a man from Macedonia who begged him to go there and help them. We have noticed before that frequently when a new geographical or cultural barrier was to be crossed by the gospel, the Spirit of God took a special initiative. So it was here as Paul and the others prepared to cross into Europe.

The second important event came when Luke joined the missionary team in Troas. We know this simply because he changes from the third person to the first person plural, from "they" to "we" in the narrative. Some think the two events were connected. Many believe Paul's "thorn (literally, 'stake') in the flesh" which caused him such distress (see 2 Cor. 12:7-9) was an illness which at times incapacitated him and brought terrible pain. They theorize that this kept him from going to Ephesus or Bithynia at this time and brought him to Troas to seek medical help. The east coast of the Aegean Sea was the home of medicine. Hippocrates and Galen were from the area. In this case God led Paul to the physician Luke, who was either already a believer or became one through the apostles. Then, the theory continues, Luke planted the concerns in the mind of Paul which became the seeds of the vision given to him.

From Troas they soon sailed to Neapolis, a seaport, and then traveled to Philippi, the major city of that part of Macedonia. The city was named for Philip of Macedon, father of Alexander the Great. William Barclay makes the fascinating observation that the area was rich in memories of Alexander who had wished to "marry the east to the west" and make the world one. His method was military conquest; his goal was to spread Greek culture everywhere.[1] Now Paul crossed the Aegean, going from east to west with a similar yet different vision of making the world one. His method was proclamation in the power of the Spirit; his goal was to share the Good News where it had not yet been heard. His ultimate expectation was "that at the name of Jesus every knee should bow . . . and every tongue confess that Jesus Christ is Lord" (Phil. 2:10,11).

The missionary team, now composed of Paul, Silas, Timothy and Luke, illustrated in itself the message that Christ had broken down the barriers between different groups and accepted all who had faith. Paul and Silas were Jews; Timothy was half-Jew, half-Greek; and now Luke, a Gentile believer, had joined them. Today we are used to hearing that "the medium is the message." Such was the case here; the composition of this missionary band pointed powerfully to the message they shared. It also indicated great cultural sensitivity by Paul and the others. The Gentiles knew the Jews looked down on them as religiously inferior. Now here was a Jewish rabbi who proclaimed a different message of equality and unity in Christ. And he proved its truth by including a Gentile as a part of the group.

Philippi

Philippi, which was to become the location of Paul's favorite church, was a Roman colony. Built up and renamed by Philip of Macedon in 356 B.C., it had seen Alexander the Great march through on his way to conquest in 335 B.C. It came under Roman control in 167 B.C. A battle on the nearby Plain of Drama in 42 B.C. changed the nature of the Roman Empire when Octavian and Anthony defeated Brutus and Cassius, the assassins of Julius Caesar. Octavian, who became known as Augustus, later defeated Anthony and Cleopatra and took control of the empire. Veterans of this battle were settled in Philippi, adding to its pride as a Roman colony. It enjoyed self-government and freedom from tribute to the emperor, and its citizens had the rights of those who lived in Italy. Its people dressed like Romans, used the Roman language and followed Roman law.

Paul normally went first to the synagogue in a new city to share the gospel with Jews and God-fearers. But 10 male, adult Jews were necessary to form a synagogue. Apparently in this city with its anti-Jewish feelings, there were not enough to do so. In such a situation it was common to have a place of prayer, usually by the river. There the local Jews, along with God-fearers, would meet on the Sabbath. Finding the place by the river, Paul and his companions joined them for prayer and worship, then told them the Good News of Jesus.

Often missionaries, visiting a place for the first time to share the gospel, encounter those who are open to the message, eager to accept it and follow Christ. The Holy Spirit has clearly been working in lives before the arrival of the messengers. This was now Paul's experience.

Lydia, a cloth merchant and a God-fearer, was present. Perhaps she had begun to worship the God of Israel in her native city, Thyatira, where there was a Jewish colony. Luke, again emphasizing God's initiative, says "The Lord opened her heart to respond to Paul's message" (Acts 16:14). She was Paul's first convert in Europe. After she and her household were baptized she was eager for Paul and the others to stay in her home. Both her business, selling the expensive purple cloth, and her hospitality, which indicated a large home, lead us to believe she had some wealth.

Thus Paul and the others had to shift their strategy somewhat in this city where there was no synagogue. Still they found a way of making contact with those whom they believed would show interest in their message. The church was formed around the nucleus of Lydia's household, including her servants and perhaps her children, and began to grow.

A Power Encounter and Prison

J. Hudson Taylor, the great founder of the China Inland Mission (now the Overseas Missionary Fellowship), once said that he never saw an advance of the gospel that was not followed by a counterattack by the adversary. That was Paul's experience and we should not think it unusual when it is ours. The attack may come because of prejudice or economic fears or for other reasons, but it will come.

The next incident Luke chooses to narrate involved a person at the opposite end of the social and economic scale. She was an exploited slave girl, demon possessed and believed to be inspired by Apollo, the god especially associated with oracles. The superstitious people, believing her sayings were the words of the god, paid her owners well to have their fortunes told. The spirit within her recognized the power and truth of

Paul's message and constantly proclaimed the fact as she followed the group day after day. Finally Paul met the power of evil with the power of God and exorcized the demon in the name of Jesus Christ. The girl was freed from her spiritual slavery.

Now her owners were wounded where it hurt the most, in their pocketbooks. The girl was not a person to them; she was an object, a tool with which to make money. They took no pleasure in her restoration; their only concern was the loss of their income. The new religion had been tolerated up to now. But when it affected their illegitimate profits, the girl's owners collected a mob, dragged Paul and Silas to the city officials in the marketplace and charged them with "unRoman" conduct.

Paul, usually denounced by the Jews as one who taught they should reject the Law of Moses, now heard himself accused of something quite different. The owners of the girl cleverly exploited the anti-Semitism of the crowd as well as their great pride in being Roman. "These men are Jews," they said, "and are throwing our city into an uproar by advocating customs unlawful for us Romans to accept or practice" (16:20,21). The crowd joined in, confusion increased and the magistrate allowed no defense from these foreign Jews. Paul and Silas were stripped and severely beaten with rods by the lichtors, attendants of the magistrates who acted as police. This was one of three times Paul would suffer such a beating (see 2 Cor. 11:25). It is worth noting that both times Luke tells of a Gentile attack on the apostles it came because the gospel had threatened illicit economic interests (see Acts 19:23-41). The gospel cuts across all kinds of selfish interests, whether they are concerned with prejudice or profit.

After the beating Paul and Silas were taken to the prison and thrown into the inner cell while their feet were fastened in stocks.

Singing Hymns at Midnight

The pain and discomfort suffered by the two missionaries was terrible. Their backs were bruised if not raw from the beating. The stocks were so constructed that their legs could be spread as far as the jailer wished, leaving the prisoners in great pain. By midnight their bodies throbbed with pain and they no doubt were hungry and thirsty as well.

But that was not the worst of it. If we know Paul and his companion at all we know their greatest concern was for the infant Philippian church. What would happen to Lydia and the other new Christians? Would they be persecuted or expelled from the city? Would they remain faithful or would they turn away from Christ? What about Luke and Timothy? They had not been dragged to the magistrates. But now would they too be taken and beaten?

As they suffered through the night in the dark inner dungeon, tortured by such pain and concern, the two must have wondered about their own fate as well. Would there be more beatings or expulsion from the city? Or worse? They had not been given opportunity to attest to their Roman citizenship the first time, perhaps they would not be heard on the next day.

In the midst of such pain, concern and uncertainty, Paul and Silas prayed and sang hymns at midnight. It was midnight not only by the clock. It seemed to be midnight for the Philippian church and perhaps for their whole mission as well. Yet the two prayed and gave audible praise to God. Did they praise God for the privilege of suffering for Christ, as the other apostles had once done (see Acts 5:41)? Did they give thanks because of their confidence that God would show His faithfulness to His people, sustain them and glorify

Himself even in this situation? No doubt both, and as they did so the other prisoners must have marveled at such faith.

God answered their prayers more quickly and dramatically than they anticipated. An earthquake threw the doors open and loosened the chains. The jailer, probably a retired soldier, saw the doors open and concluded that the prisoners had escaped. Since he was accountable for all of them he could only think of one way out—suicide. Paul must have seen his silhouette in the open doorway, sword in hand, about to plunge it into his body. He shouted, "Don't harm yourself! We are all here!" (Acts 16:28).

What kind of men were these two prisoners? the jailer wondered. They praised their God in the most difficult circumstances. Apparently their example kept the other prisoners from escaping. Now they were concerned to save the life of the jailer whom they would normally see as their enemy. The old soldier could not understand it. There must be some great power in the new religion they preached.

The jailer called for lights, brought Paul and Silas out and asked, "What must I do to be saved?" (v. 30). What did he mean by his question? Was he concerned only for physical safety? There were many religions at this time which promised salvation of one kind or another. He might have heard the slave girl shout that the two were telling the way to be saved. Whatever his level of understanding when he asked the question, the answer was far simpler than he had imagined, while the salvation was much deeper. "Believe in the Lord Jesus, and you will be saved—you and your household" (v. 31), was the succinct answer. After that Paul and Silas explained the way more completely.

The jailer washed their wounds, took them into his house and fed them. Then he and his family were baptized. The ancient preacher Chrysostom put it beautifully, "He washed and was washed. He washed them from their stripes and he himself was washed from his sin."

Thus Luke tells of three people changed by the power of Christ in Philippi: Lydia, a wealthy merchant; a demon-possessed slave girl; and a middle-class government functionary. The three, coming from opposite ends as well as the middle of the socio-economic spectrum, show us graphically the inclusiveness of the Body of Christ. Jews and Gentiles, wealthy merchant, Roman jailer and slave girl, there was room for all.

Luke also tells us that the households of both Lydia and the jailer were baptized. We do not know all who were included in them, but probably there were both family and servants. We live in a society which emphasizes individualism. But the experience of the early believers suggests that we give greater importance to the need for solidarity and mutual support within both family and church. We do not enter the Christian life without the witness and encouragement of other believers. We cannot live effective Christian lives without their support either.

The next day the magistrates, perhaps knowing they had acted unjustly, ordered the release of Paul and Silas. But the two refused to go. Their beating was against the law. They were Roman citizens and a citizen could not be beaten. The magistrate, alarmed at the discovery that they were citizens, came to the prison and apologized. Only then did Paul and Silas agree to leave. However, they first met with the church in Lydia's house and encouraged the believers. Their manner of dealing with the magistrates was probably less for personal satisfaction than for the sake of the believers. The city officials would not be so quick to act against the church next time. Paul and Silas went on to

Thessalonica, apparently leaving Luke and Timothy to continue the ministry in Philippi.

Once more the Spirit had led them to share the gospel in a new circle. God once more turned persecution and apparent tragedy into a new advance. Now this new area of penetration would soon be enlarged as Paul and Silas continued on to other areas of Greece.

Questions for Discussion

1. How would you analyze the disagreement between Paul and Barnabas? Who was right and who was wrong? Could it be that both fulfilled useful functions in Mark's life?

2. Was Paul inconsistent in having Timothy circumcised? Explain the difference between Paul's understanding of the function of circumcision in this case and that of the "circumcision party" in Acts 15.

3. It is clear that God used a number of different ways to guide His servants in Acts. List as many as you can. In what ways has God guided you?

4. Can you think of some ministries that would benefit by including an interracial or intercultural team in them? Would such situations be found only overseas or might they be in your own country or community?

5. Have you ever reached a "midnight" in your life? Did you see God work? How?

6. If someone asked you the jailer's question, how would you answer? Then how would you explain what your answer meant?

Note

1. William Barclay, *The Acts of the Apostles*, The Daily Study Bible series (Edinburgh: The Saint Andrew Press, 1962), pp. 131,132.

CHAPTER ELEVEN

Strength in the Storm

Acts 27:1—28:10

If a Hollywood producer wanted to base a movie on a great tale of action, he could do no better than to film the story of this shipwreck. It has all the elements of adventure: a terrifying storm, days and nights of darkness and despair, the narrowest of escapes from death, and the final rescue of all on board. The drama has a unique twist. The hero is not some swashbuckling sailor, the ship's captain, or even the Roman officer in charge. It is a Jewish rabbi! The rabbi, now a far-ranging preacher of Jesus Christ, takes charge at the crucial hour leading all on board to safety. Most people might think it too unlikely to be true, but it happened.

Luke's eyewitness account of this event is one of the most graphic pieces of descriptive writing in ancient literature. His great care as an historian is evident here. A number of writers, familiar with the ancient world, have attested to the accuracy of Luke's description of trade routes, ships and weather conditions.

But before following Paul and his companions across the Mediterranean through the storm to shipwreck on the beach at Malta, we will review briefly the portion of Acts 17 to 26 which must be left out of this study.

Thessalonica to Jerusalem
After leaving Philippi on his second missionary jour-

ney, Paul continued on to Thessalonica, Berea and
other Greek cities, leaving nuclei of believers in each
place. Then he spent a brief time in Ephesus before
returning to Antioch. On his third journey he revisited
Galatia, then went to Ephesus for an extended ministry
of over two years. During this period of solid growth
Paul made a fateful decision: he must go to Jerusalem
(see Acts 19:21). He would go to reassure the leaders
there of the effectiveness and validity of the mission to
the Gentiles. In so doing he hoped to emphasize and
strengthen the unity of the church. To symbolize their
oneness he would take with him a number of Gentile
converts bearing gifts from their churches to aid the
poor in Jerusalem. He knew the trip involved great risk,
the danger of attack from unbelieving Jews and even
the possibility of rejection by the Jerusalem believers.
The fact that he chose to go anyway indicates the
importance he attached to the venture. After Jerusalem
he intended to go to Rome and then on to Spain.

Luke's space was limited so he had to select carefully the incidents he would relate. Then why did he
devote seven and one-half chapters, one-fourth of the
book, to Paul's final visit to Jerusalem and his trip to
Rome? We are not told of any new converts or
churches established. Yet Luke considered these
events of the greatest importance. We need to ask
what the incidents in the two cities represented in the
overall scheme of things.

The events in Jerusalem proved that despite the
conciliatory actions of Paul, official Judaism would continue its rejection of any gospel which proclaimed
acceptance of the Gentiles equally with Jews (see Acts
22:21-23; 23:1-22). Many individual Jews would believe
but the nation as a whole would not. It would guard to
the bitter end its narrow conviction that only those who
kept the Law were acceptable to God. There was no

way they could accept that the followers of the Messiah would ever become a universal church which included men and women of every race, language and culture.

Because of this intransigence Paul was tried by the mob, the Jewish council and the secular rulers, all of whom rejected his message. Perhaps some might believe in Jesus as the Jewish Messiah, but it is clear they could not tolerate the mission to the Gentiles. The only way Paul could save his life and continue his mission was to appeal to Caesar. As a result he was taken from Jerusalem, the Jewish center, to Rome, the Gentile capital. What would he find there? Another closed door or the gateway to the rest of the world?

From Caesarea to Crete

Having appealed to Caesar to avoid being sent to sure death in Jerusalem, Paul was sent to Rome by the governor, Festus. He had spent two years as a prisoner in Caesarea since his visit to Jerusalem. Some believe that Luke remained near Paul during this period but took advantage of the opportunity to interview people and gather the material from which he wrote his gospel.

It was already mid-August. Soon the time would be past for safe travel; Paul and several other prisoners were put into the hand of Julius, a centurion. Julius was one of a special group of officers who acted as couriers between Rome and its armies and at times conducted prisoners to Rome. He must have been a man of considerable experience and ability. Aristarchus and Luke accompanied Paul. Some scholars have suggested that the only way they could have done so under Roman custom at the time was to be registered as Paul's slaves. If so, they were willing to go to any lengths to remain with the apostle as he faced his ordeal in Rome. Others contend that Paul would not have allowed such a demeaning act. They suggest that because of the apostle's importance as one who had appealed to Caesar, he was given the privilege of taking his friends with him.

They embarked from Caesarea in a small coastal vessel and sailed 69 miles north to Sidon, where Paul was allowed to visit the church. Then bucking the prevailing winds from the west and northwest they sailed east and north of Cyprus to the south coast of Asia Minor. From there, heading for the most part into the prevailing wind, the small craft slowly made its way west along the coast, utilizing local breezes and the westward sea current. Passing Cilicia and Pamphylia they reached Myra, an important port in southern Asia Minor. This was one of the main ports for the grain ships which regularly sailed from Alexandria to Rome. One of those ships was in port and to it Julius transferred his soldiers and prisoners.

The grain ship was perhaps 140 feet long and 36 feet wide. It was difficult to handle with one large square sail, guided by two steering oars instead of a rudder. It could not sail directly into the west wind toward Italy. Making its way slowly, it followed a tortuous route to Cnidus, then around the eastern tip of Crete along the south coast of the island. With difficulty because of unfavorable winds, they were able to reach a small bay called Fair Havens.

The Storm

Because of the delays it was now too late in the year to travel safely. The Fast, the Day of Atonement of the Jews, had already passed. Sailing was considered dangerous after mid-October. A decision had to be made. Should they stay the winter in Fair Havens or try to make a larger port with greater protection from the winds? A council was held in which Paul was invited to take part. The centurion, as the senior officer present, made the final decision. Disregarding the advice of Paul he followed the council of the ship owner and pilot who thought they could wait for a favorable wind and reach the better harbor at Phoenix.

When a gentle south wind began to blow they quickly weighed anchor and set full sail west along the coast. It should have been only a few hours of sailing. But soon a gale of hurricane force came from the northeast off the 7,000 foot peaks of the island, caught the ship broadside and drove it into the open sea. Nothing could be done to control the vessel. Everything was soon in confusion and chaos.

Briefly in the lee of a small island, called Cauda, they were able to haul the lifeboat on board to prevent its being broken against the ship. Next they passed cables, already in place, around the ship as a safety measure. An ancient writer said a typhoon like this one was capable of breaking a ship's hull apart. The captain and the crew took every measure they could think of. Their greatest fear was that they would be driven onto the shoals off North Africa and be destroyed. They lowered the sea anchor and ran with the wind. But with no letup in the storm during the next two days, they threw much of the ship's cargo overboard.

As the gale continued at full force it blotted out both stars and sun, leaving no way of determining the ship's position. Running out of control, taking on water, the vessel was in danger either of sinking in the open sea or being dashed to pieces on some rocky shore. Imagine the terror. Exhausted from battling the storm, nauseated from sea sickness, weak from hunger and demoralized by fear, they lost all hope of being saved.

Paul Takes Leadership

All but Paul! Now the prisoner becomes the leader. In Philippi Paul sang hymns of praise in the prison at midnight. Now as the ship and its crew reached their own "midnight," the apostle sang a different "hymn" to the glory of God. After an all-too-human "I told you so," he exhorted them, "Keep up your courage, because not one of you will be lost" (see Acts 27:21,22).

Paul had known the terror of storms before. He had survived three shipwrecks and, on one occasion, a day and night clinging to a spar in the open sea (see 2 Cor. 11:25). But experience was not his reason for hope. God, to whom he belonged and whom he served so well, had assured him two years earlier that he was to bear witness in Rome (see Acts 23:11). Now He had again stood beside Paul and repeated the promise. The apostle would stand trial before Caesar and God would give him the lives of all on board. He concluded with a ringing affirmation of faith, "I believe God that it will happen just as He told me" (see Acts 27:25).

We remember Winston Churchill encouraging, exhorting the English people at their darkest hour in 1940. In the heat of the apparently hopeless battle he was convinced that England would survive and persevere to victory. And the confidence he showed so powerfully became an essential factor in bringing about that victory. So it was with Paul. His own confidence in God, proclaimed powerfully in the midst of despair, became the essential factor in their survival.

Why did the prisoner become the leader, the catalyst of change in this situation when all others had lost hope? Clearly it was the quality of Paul's faith. I believe this story gives us one of the greatest demonstrations and definitions of faith in the entire Bible. All of us, no matter where we are in our Christian pilgrimage, have much to learn from the deep, robust faith of Paul which sustained him in the storm.

The Nature of Paul's Faith

Paul had given himself unreservedly to God as he

met Him in Jesus Christ, but his faith had not come easily. Attempting to serve God as a strict Pharisee, he had struggled and known failure within (see Rom. 7). He had rejected the claim that Jesus was the Messiah. Only a personal encounter with the risen Lord brought him to surrender.

The intensity of Paul's struggle and the nature of his conversion led him to face squarely the issues involved. Jesus was Lord, alive and powerful in the world. God was not a passive relic of the past; He was actively working in the present to carry out His redemptive purpose. That purpose was to send His messengers to all peoples—every race, nation, language and culture— telling them the Good News and inviting them to new life in Christ. The Lordship of Christ, His power and His purpose, now brought Paul direction and motivation.

Thus, in the first place, Paul's faith was not passive; it was constantly active. Just as he had discovered the definitive combination of God's love and power demonstrated in the cross and resurrection, he had also found that he could trust his Lord in every situation. The Lord who loved him—no matter what—would work out His purpose in every circumstance—no matter what.

Paul had seen this in prison, in beatings, stonings, mob scenes and trials of all kinds. He knew he could trust God even on a ship out of control, lost, in the midst of a gale. God told him he would get to Rome; now His messenger promised that all on board would be rescued. Paul believed God and acted accordingly.

Secondly, Paul's faith was a constantly unfolding relationship with his Lord. One of his favorite phrases was "in Christ" (see Rom. 8:1; Eph. 1:1). A Christian was one who was "in Christ." The term pointed to many aspects of the new life; its meaning was indeed almost inexhaustible. But among other things it indicated the growing nature of Christian discipleship.

In keeping with this understanding of the Christian life, Paul's goal was to "know" Christ, the power of His resurrection and the fellowship of His suffering and death (see Phil. 3:10). At first glance this statement may seem a contradiction of Paul's whole life of discipleship. If anyone ever gave evidence of "knowing" Christ, demonstrating His power and sharing in His suffering, Paul did. But he realized that there was more to know of Christ's person, purpose, power, compassion and grace. The life "in Christ" could never be static any more than it could be passive.

Thirdly, Paul's faith was focused not on himself but on God's will for His creation. He had given himself fully to his Lord's purpose for the world. This was no self-centered faith constantly asking what the personal benefits would be. Many of us may begin there, but one sure sign of Christian maturity comes when we shift our focus and ask how God will be served and glorified in a specific situation. Another way of putting it is to say that Paul's goal here was not survival, but mission. Eternal life assured, his personal safety or survival was not the primary issue; rather it was the mission God had given him (see Phil. 1:20-25). As we have already noted, Paul's specific goal at this time was to preach in Rome, help build up the believers there and encourage them to become the base for his mission to Spain (see Rom. 15:23-29). His long-term goal was to contribute in every way possible to God's own purpose, "That all nations might believe and obey him" (Rom. 16:26). Michelangelo once said, "It is only well with me when I have a chisel in my hand." Paul might have said, "It is only well with me when I am pushing on to proclaim the gospel to those who have not heard."

Thus Paul's faith was active not passive, growing not static, and focused on God and His world, not on himself. It was this kind of faith which delivered him from fear during the storm and catapulted him into leadership when all others had fallen into despair.

The Shipwreck

Nearing midnight on the fourteenth night of the storm, the sailors found they were moving into more shallow waters and approaching land. They dropped four anchors in an attempt to halt the drift of the ship to shore and destruction. Then under the guise of putting out more anchors they tried to escape in the lifeboat. Again Paul took leadership, warning the centurion that they would need the skills of the seamen if all were to escape. So the soldiers cut the boat loose.

Again Paul showed an impressive combination of faith and practical wisdom. They had eaten little in two weeks. They were weak and ill-equipped to meet the ordeal ahead. So Paul insisted they all eat and encouraged them, repeating his assurance that all would survive. Then "he took some bread and gave thanks to God in front of them all . . . broke it and began to eat" (Acts 27:35). Paul's act and Luke's description of it remind us of the Lord's Supper (see 1 Cor. 11:23,24). Obviously this was not such a celebration in any formal sense. But Paul and the other believers present could not help but be reminded of the many other occasions and circumstances in which they had given thanks and broken bread in celebration of the Lord's death and resurrection. Now the act was a powerful reminder of Christ's victory over every evil power and His presence with them, even in the storm.

After all had eaten they lightened the ship by throwing the cargo overboard. When daylight came they cut the anchors loose and let the ship run, hoping for a safe landing on the beach. But it ran aground and was broken up by the pounding surf. Knowing they would be held responsible for any who escaped, the soldiers wanted to kill all the prisoners. Again Paul's influence was crucial. His leadership had been instrumental in saving many of those on board. Now the centurion wanted to save the apostle's life. He prevented the soldiers from killing anyone and all eventually made it safely to shore.

On Malta

They were well received by the islanders and soon a fire was burning to warm the exhausted travelers. Luke notes that Paul began to gather sticks for the fire. Here is another unforgettable picture of the apostle, as impressive as his act of giving hope in the midst of the storm. If anyone had earned the right to rest and receive the attention and accolades of the others it was Paul! But once ashore he quietly began to perform the next task at hand, menial or not.

The picture of Paul picking up sticks, put alongside Paul acting in the middle of the storm, gives us a model of Christian leadership. He trusted God in the crisis and was not afraid to say so. He was not afraid to point to the source of his confidence and strength. He had no blueprint showing exactly what would happen. But he trusted God completely, said so and acted on his faith.

His trust in God freed him to be concerned for the needs of others and led him to the menial task. The hero of the rescue showed no concern for status, no feeling that he had already done enough. He looked for the next job to be done and did it.

A third aspect of Paul's leadership was that it motivated others to fulfill their own responsibilities. The centurion had final authority in this situation, while Paul was only a prisoner. But it was the apostle's example of concern for the well-being of all that led the Roman officer to fulfill his duty, preventing the sailors from escaping and the soldiers from killing the prisoners.

Paul's ministry continued. Despite weariness he lost no time in healing the sick, including the father of Malta's leading citizen. We can imagine these acts were accompanied by the news of Christ.

Paul was now on the last lap of his journey to Rome, the center of the empire and capital of the world as he knew it. Even though the church already existed there, Paul's arrival marked the ending of one journey and the beginning of another. The journey of the gospel from Jerusalem to Rome symbolized the transformation of the church from a small group within Judaism to the universal Body of Christ which it would become. The second journey would take the Good News out from the Mediterranean world and Graeco-Roman culture to the ends of the earth until the church included men and women of every nation, race, language, and culture.

Questions for Discussion

1. In your opinion, why did most Jews reject the gospel? What were the main reasons? Are there aspects of the gospel message which you are tempted to reject? Why? How do you deal with them?

2. Analyze the nature of Paul's leadership in the storm. Write down every element which contributed to it. What does this teach you not only about Christian leadership but the Christian life in general?

3. Analyze the nature of Paul's faith for yourself. What new elements do you discover here which contribute to your personal definition of faith?

4. List all the things which the phrase "in Christ" means to you.

5. Compare Paul in the storm with Paul in Malta. What additional lessons about Christian leadership and life-style do you see there?

CHAPTER TWELVE

Getting Our Acts Together

Acts 28 (and 29)

About mid-February when travel was safe again, Paul and his companions were put aboard another Alexandrian grain ship which had wintered in Malta. They sailed to Syracuse, on Sicily's east coast, then to Rhegium, on the Italian mainland across the strait from Messina. From there it took another day to reach Puteoli, the most sheltered point in southern Italy, where the grain ships unloaded their cargos. There was a church in the city, possibly founded by a merchant, sailor or government official who had heard the gospel during his travels.

By this time, through the witness of many unknown believers and perhaps missionary bands as well, there were churches in a number of important Italian cities. Paul must have welcomed the opportunity to spend a week with the brethren in Puteoli. No doubt he eagerly asked what they knew of Rome's official attitude toward Christians as well as the viewpoint Jewish leaders took toward the church.

It was a journey of 140 miles following the famed Appian Way to Rome. We can imagine the emotions chasing each other within Paul's mind as he approached the city which had been his goal for so long (see Rom. 1:11-13). His forthcoming trial before Caesar was probably not his greatest concern. The questions in his mind no doubt focused on the progress of the gospel. What would he find in the church there? How strong and bold would it be? What of its attitude toward him and his understanding of the universal scope of the gospel? Had the Roman church accepted and understood his letter written to them two years earlier? Would the believers support his passion to take the Good News beyond Rome to Spain? Or would Judaizing influence be found among them, leading them to reject Paul?

And what of the Jewish community? There were at least 9, perhaps as many as 11, synagogues in Rome, with a Jewish population between 10 and 20 thousand. Would these Jews, more accustomed to the Gentile world than those in Jerusalem, be more open to the gospel and its universal message?

Some of the apostle's questions were answered when one delegation of believers met him at the Forum of Appius, 43 miles from the city, and another joined them at Three Taverns, 10 miles closer. Their presence encouraged Paul greatly and he gave thanks to God. Their long journey on foot to meet him must have indicated their endorsement of his ministry.

In Rome: Encounter with the Jews

The commander of the Praetorian Guard from 51 to 62 A.D. was Afranius Burrus, known as a fair and honest man. This may have been the reason why Paul was allowed to live in a house at his own expense. The only reminder that he was a prisoner was the chain that bound him to a soldier day and night. It did not happen in the way he planned, but Paul's dream that he would preach the gospel in Rome was about to be fulfilled.

Losing no time after he was situated in a house, Paul requested that the Jewish leaders visit him. He was anxious to discover their attitude toward him, still more eager to proclaim his message to them.

Two concerns were in Paul's mind as he met the Jewish leaders. First, there was the accusation against him by the Jerusalem Jews which had prompted his appeal to Caesar. Had it been sent on to Rome; did the local Jews plan to pursue the case? Secondly, what would their attitude be toward the gospel? If the Jewish community in Rome believed in Jesus as Messiah and began to understand the barrier-breaking implications of the gospel, it would be a great step forward. Perhaps they could reach some of the Jewish communities which had rejected Paul.

Thus for both reasons the apostle eagerly stated that he was not unfaithful to the Jewish people or their traditions and had no charge to bring against them. Then he made his main point. He was there, bound with a chain, because of the hope of Israel, the same hope for which those before him prayed and waited.

The Jews' reply was diplomatic and noncommittal. They had received no accusations from Judea against Paul, not even any bad reports against him personally. Apparently the Judean leaders had dropped the case. However, they added, people everywhere were speaking against this "sect." Still, they said, they were ready to hear Paul's views.

The second meeting included a much larger number. All day long Paul expounded the Scriptures, no doubt amidst intense debate, showing how the Old Testament writings had been fulfilled in Jesus, the Messiah. The Kingdom of God had dawned, but it was far greater in scope than that which they had expected.

Some believed; others—probably a majority—could not admit that God would do something so much greater than their traditions anticipated. Like the Jews elsewhere they chose to reject the message. With a heavy heart Paul quoted God's words to the young Isaiah, warning him that his own people would close

their ears and refuse to listen (see Isa. 6:9,10). Now
once again they refused to hear the messenger of God.
Tragically, none are as blind as those who refuse to see,
none as deaf as those who refuse to hear. Now God
would send His salvation to the Gentiles. They would
listen!

The rejection of the gospel by the Jews would
always remain a mystery and a burden for Paul and for
us. No one would ever fully understand it in this life.
But as Paul had previously written to the Roman believers, the rejection by the Jews had forced the church out
into the Gentile world with the gospel. Jewish rejection
was an important, perhaps even an essential factor, in
leading the church to break with Jewish culture, freeing
it to take root eventually in every other culture of mankind. Even so, God was still not through with His special people (see Rom. 11:11-32).

Paul's Ministry in Rome

How we wish Luke had told us more about the next
two years and the rest of Paul's life. But we do know he
had two full years of ministry in Rome, probably from
59 to 61. We know he continued his extended ministry
through his letters, writing Colossians, Philemon,
Ephesians, and Philippians during this period. In them
he dealt both with great theological issues and with personal matters.

In Colossians Paul dealt with the person of Christ,
the Head of the church. In Ephesians he expounded on
the church as the Body of Christ in which the ancient
barriers separating different peoples had been shattered. In Philemon he dealt with the personal problems
of a runaway slave, potentially under a death sentence,
who first found Paul, then found Christ in Rome. He
wrote Philippians to express thanks for gifts sent him
and to clear up other matters. It is one of Paul's most

joyful writings. In it he expresses confidence that God is using even his chains to advance the gospel.

Members of the palace guard, chained to him one after the other, could not help but become acquainted with the Good News. Most believers in the city were made bolder in their witness by Paul's example.

When Paul was not teaching those who came to him from Rome and its environs he spent many hours with his close friends, no doubt leading them into deeper understanding of the faith and encouraging them in their ministries. The letters he wrote during this period mention a number of them: Tychicus, Timothy, Epaphroditus, Aristarchus, Mark, Luke, and others. His influence on the lives of these men helped lay the foundation for the next generation of leadership.

Luke says that without hindrance Paul proclaimed the Kingdom of God and the Lordship of Christ to all who came to him, and no doubt many did. Can you imagine how many believers attempting to share the Good News with friends must have brought them to Paul? The message no doubt made a powerful impact in Nero's Rome, where Caesar was said to be a god and the power of the empire was seen everywhere.

Here Luke ends his narrative. Various theories have been put forth to explain why he went no further. The simplest is that he had achieved his goal. He had shown how the gospel was taken from Jerusalem the Jewish center, to Rome the Gentile capital. He traced each step as the Spirit unfolded the broader implications of the message and the church grew from a sect within Judaism to the universal Body of Christ.

This was Luke's goal. It was not to picture the whole career of Paul any more than it was to describe all of Peter's ministry. It is probable that after two years the charges against Paul were dropped for lack of accusers and he was released.

In that case, Paul had three more years of ministry after his release, but we know almost nothing about him during this period. There is some evidence that he went to Spain. Most certainly he wrote his letters to Titus and Timothy at this time. We have no reason to doubt the ancient tradition which says the apostle was finally beheaded in Rome on the orders of Nero in 64 A.D. Most believe that Peter perished at the same time.

Acts: An Unfinished Book

The narrative ends with Paul proclaiming the gospel in Rome. As we have indicated, Luke's objective was to describe the process by which the Spirit led an often reluctant church as it began to fulfill Jesus' mandate to be His "witnesses . . . to the ends of the earth." Luke achieved his goal in magnificent fashion, but in a deeper sense the very manner of Acts' ending points to a new and even greater beginning. The book describes one important phase of the history of the church, but that history is far from complete. As it now stands, it is like an Agatha Christie mystery with the last chapter missing. The end of the story, chapter 29 of Acts, remains to be told. And you and I are called to become participants as God continues to write the history of the Acts of the risen Christ who leads His people as they take the Good News to the ends of the earth.

Thus Acts stands as a perpetual challenge to our concept of the church and its task. On a mountain overlooking the great fortress in Cartagena, Columbia, stands an old monastery. Built in the seventeenth century to house Augustinian monks who were to take the Catholic faith to the peoples of the region, it later was abandoned and fell into disrepair. When I visited there in 1976 I read a plaque which told how early in the century the government wished to restore and preserve the ancient buildings as a monument to the colonial past. Columbian leaders promised to rebuild the ruins if the church would send back a group of monks to live there and, in the words of the inscription, "Take care of this historic relic."

That describes the picture that many still have of the church of Jesus Christ. They see it as an "historic relic": defender of an ideology, of certain values, or just a monument to be preserved for the sake of nostalgia.

Even though we may not fall into these errors, all of us are in constant danger of becoming content with a view of the church which is much less than God's plan.

The only remedy is to live constantly with the Scriptures, both the Old and New Testaments, to find there what God wants His church to be. Returning again to Genesis 12:3 we are reminded that at the dawn of redemptive history His plan was that, through the descendants of Abraham, *all* the families of the earth would be blessed. And all believers in Christ are spiritual descendants of Abraham. We look at one of the greatest prophecies of the Messiah and discover again that He would be a light to the ends of the earth (see Isa. 49:6). We remember that the church is the messianic community through which He carries out His mission in history. We look again at the mandate of the risen Lord, "Go and make disciples of all the *ethne*, every cultural, linguistic, racial, and ethnic group on earth" (see Matt. 28:19). Then we come to Jesus' words recorded by Luke, "You will be my witnesses . . . to the ends of the earth" (Acts 1:8).

Reviewing Acts we see that the first result of the gifts of the Holy Spirit was that everyone "heard," in his own native language, the "wonders of God" (Acts 2:8-11). We followed the Spirit's work as He fought off every attempt to limit the gospel to one circle or another. We watched Him lead a reluctant church out of its native territory and culture, toppling one barrier after another as Samaritan, Ethiopian, God-fearer, pagan, Greek, and Roman heard and believed.

We are led inescapably to the conviction that God's primary agenda for His church is that, led by the same Spirit, it should continue to take the Good News to every unique cultural group on earth.

Acts and Christian Discipleship

A serious study of Acts cannot leave us with an easy view of the Christian life which focuses on ourselves and the blessings God gives us. It changes our agenda. Many, perhaps most American Christians have never allowed the gospel to challenge their personal goals. Their primary ambitions are unchanged by their faith in Christ and their profession of His Lordship. But Acts challenges us to adopt God's agenda for His world as our own. Because He continues to act today, the greatest privilege of the Christian life is to be a participant with Him in His saving work in history.

We note that the New Testament terms used to describe God's people are dynamic, action-oriented, not passive. One of the best known is *disciple* or learner. We know from watching Jesus and the Twelve that a disciple was not one who sat in a classroom while the teacher poured facts and ideas into him. He was active, a disciple-follower who learned as he followed and followed as he learned. He watched his Master minister to people, listened to the explanation of His actions, heard Him teach and went out to do the same.

Followers of the Way (see Acts 9:2; 22:4) was another term which described the early believers. It obviously describes people actively following a particular life-style, headed in the direction which God has set for His people and for history. *Christ-iani*, those belonging to the party of Christ, was the nickname contemptuously given in Antioch. It implies that believers not only profess to belong to Christ but have adopted His goals for themselves and for the world. Peter's clear statement of God's purpose for His church reinforces this. We are a "people belonging to God" that we might "declare the praises of him who called us out of darkness into his marvelous light" (1 Pet. 2:9).

Thus Acts teaches us to beware of three great temptations which have befallen the church throughout its history. The first is that of the Jewish nation which assumed that the gifts and blessings of God were for them alone. We often forget, just as ancient Israel did, that God called Abraham and all his descendants, physical and spiritual, so that through them all the families of the earth would be blessed. Too often we jealously clutch God's gifts to our breasts, fiercely protecting ourselves, fearful of any whose voices might intrude on our comfort. I think of one affluent American denomination whose members give an average of three dollars yearly to meet human need and proclaim the gospel around the world—about the price of a quick trip (for one) to MacDonald's!

Secondly, we easily fall into the sin of the Jewish leaders who confronted the apostles and forbade them to preach. Conservators of the traditions of the nation, they believed God had done mighty saving works in the past; some even hoped He would do so again in the future; but they refused to believe God was active and powerful in the present. They maintained monuments to a god who was an absentee landlord at best, or dead at worst. But Acts presents us with an active God, sometimes working through dramatic miracles, signs and wonders, sometimes quietly in the inner life.

His power is the same today and his goals are the same as well, that men and women everywhere might receive the new life. This suggests that we are called to discover what God is doing in our communities and world, ask Him to show us how we are to participate, then expect to see Him work in power.

Thirdly, we must be careful not to follow the Judaizers who believed that all others must adopt Jewish culture and become like them before they could follow Christ. This is not only an issue for those who go to cultures other than their own; it is a question for the dominant group in any society as it seeks to evangelize ethnic minorities; it is a need for older believers to consider as they communicate the gospel to another generation. It will always be an issue for the church. The gospel is not to be cemented rigidly within one particular culture so that the two become inseparable. All of us are constantly called to distinguish between the Good News and the forms in which we received it if we are to become better communicators.

A Definition of "Christian" for Today

I suggest we go back to the drawing board (for us, the Scriptures) and seek to redefine the term *Christian* for today. Most of our current definitions are oriented toward our inner life and our personal needs. We are much like the church which, after a few years, settled down in Jerusalem and forgot Jesus' mandate to go to all the world. Acts shows us how the Spirit led a hesitant church out from its native territory and culture, away from the exclusive focus on its own needs, to the world beyond. This is a model for the life of every believer and every church. Most of us began our Christian lives focusing on the gifts God offers us. This is legitimate at the beginning. But we are not to remain at that point in our pilgrimage any more than the church was to remain exclusively in Jerusalem. The greatest step of maturity in the Christian life comes when we no longer focus primarily on the way God will meet our own needs, but fix our attention and ambitions on His purpose for history.

With this in mind, I suggest this as a working definition: A Christian, or disciple of Jesus Christ, is one who trusts Him so much that He seeks to make God's agenda for the world the top priority in his life. That agenda is that all the *ethne* might hear the Good News and become followers of Christ.

Acts: The Story Continues

Recently I saw a statement by a secular writer to this effect: "Thank goodness, the missionary movement is coming to an end!" Nothing could be further from the truth! The risen Christ continues to write chapter 29 of His acts today. It would take another book to begin to describe all that is happening in Christian mission. A whole new era has begun. The Christian mission is now the most international, interracial and intercultural movement in history. Never before has *any* message ever been proclaimed by so many ambassadors from so many different nations, races and cultures. Nor has *any* message ever been heard and believed by so many and varied peoples.

Increasing numbers of highly motivated and gifted youth from North America and Europe are involved. But the most exciting development lies in the growing ranks of missionaries from nations which have traditionally been only on the receiving end of missions. In 1973 a team of researchers from Fuller Seminary's School of World Mission found that there were nearly 3,000 missionaries in the world from third-world nations working in cultures other than their own. Recent research by a doctoral student in the same institution now puts the number at 20,000! These include capable men and women from Korea, Nigeria, Brazil, Kenya and many other nations who cross national or tribal or linguistic barriers to share the gospel. The Nagas in northeast India train and send missionaries to neighboring nations as well as tribes within India. The Mizos, also in northern India, have sent 400 missionaries into Hindu India. Over 25 years ago they sent evangelists into the Chin Hills in Burma; now the church which grew up as a result sends its own evangelists to other tribal groups. The story continues. There is not space to tell it here.

The God whom we see in action in the book of Acts is as active today as then. His agenda is the same; so is His power. The command of the risen Christ that the Good News would be taken to the ends of the earth continues as our mandate today. Much is happening. Much remains to be done. Churches have been established in about 16,000 ethnic groups. But scholars estimate there are still 16,000 more without the gospel. If we adopt God's agenda as our own, the only remaining question is, where and how does God want us to become involved as He continues to write Acts 29?

Questions for Discussion

1. Has your understanding of the gospel changed in this study? How?

2. Has your understanding of God's purpose in history expanded? How has that changed your understanding of the church and its purpose?

3. How has studying Acts changed your understanding of the Christian life?

4. In your study of Acts, what have you learned about the Holy Spirit, His power and His purpose?

5. Has your study of Acts made an impact on the way you wish to use your gifts and possessions and on your personal goals? How?

A Brief Bibliography

The Holy Spirit

Green, Michael. *I Believe in the Holy Spirit.* Grand Rapids: Wm. B. Eerdmans Publishing Co., 1975.

Howard, David. *By the Power of the Holy Spirit.* Downers Grove, IL: InterVarsity Press, 1977.

Stott, John R.W. *Baptism and Fullness, the Work of the Holy Spirit Today.* Downers Grove, IL: InterVarsity Press, 1976.

The Book of Acts

Barclay, William. *The Acts of the Apostles.* The Daily Study Bible series. Edinburgh: Saint Andrew's Press, 1962.

Bruce, F.F. *The Book of Acts.* Grand Rapids: Wm. B. Eerdmans Publishing Co., 1956.

La Sor, William S. *Church Alive.* Ventura, CA: Regal Books, 1972.

Rackham, Richard. *The Acts of the Apostles.* London: Methuen and Company, 1901.

Stagg, Frank. *The Book of Acts.* Nashville: Broadman Press, 1955.

Winn, A.C. *The Acts of the Apostles.* Richmond: John Knox Press, 1960.